# The Tyranny
# of Public Discourse

## Abraham Lincoln's Six-Element Antidote for
## Meaningful and Persuasive Writing

*To Steve Conrad,*

*David Hirsch*

*Dan Van Haften*

## David Hirsch and Dan Van Haften

**SB**

Savas Beatie

California

Cataloging-in-Publication Data is available from the Library of Congress.

First hardcover edition, first printing:
ISBN-13: 978-1-61121-474-1
eISBN: 978-1-94066-992-2

First trade paperback edition, first printing:
ISBN-13: 978-1-61121-497-0

SB
Savas Beatie
989 Governor Drive, Suite 102
El Dorado Hills, CA 95762
Phone: 916-941-6896
(E-mail) sales@savasbeatie.com
(Web) www.savasbeatie.com

Savas Beatie titles are available at special discounts for bulk purchases in the United States by corporations, institutions, and other organizations. For more details, please contact Special Sales, P.O. Box 4527, El Dorado Hills, CA 95762. You may also e-mail us at sales@savasbeatie.com, or click over for a visit to our website at www.savasbeatie.com for additional information.

# CONTENTS

# Pyramids

# PREFACE

We recently added a question when we engage audiences: "Are you satisfied with the current state of public discourse?"

The uniform response is a loud and emphatic "No."

The reply is always the same, regardless of politics. Today's public discourse typically starts with a "conclusion" and goes downhill from there. If there are talking heads, argument begins instantly and typically runs in circles. This is a dangerous path for a society that depends upon civility and virtue to survive.

This book can teach anyone how to use logic and reason to create persuasive writing. A byproduct of this is the civility that will ensue with an elevated public discourse. *The Tyranny of Public Discourse: Abraham Lincoln's Six-Element Antidote for Meaningful and Persuasive Writing* establishes the six elements of a proposition as a verbal form of the scientific method. That might sound difficult to understand. It is not. And as you will soon see, this book sets it all out, step-by-step, from beginning to end.

# Acknowledgments

Jerry Courtney, Aaron Goldsmith, and Bill Funchion requested a path to internalize the persuasive structure of the six elements of a proposition. Thanks for identifying the need. Bill also commented on an early draft.

We thank Bic Bakkum for reading early drafts, Lylea Critelli for creative suggestions, Nick Critelli for being Nick, Jerry Courtney for unending enthusiasm, and Scott Koslow for asking the right questions.

Tony Livernois provided structural suggestions, Susan VanHaften found bumps in early versions of the text. Rod Mackler was a steady head. Shuky Meyer gave critical technical suggestions.

We thank James Cornelius for valuable advice, Dan Weinberg for unique knowledge, Bjorn Skaptason for questions and encouragement, Frank Williams for invaluable assistance, and Ted Savas for his unique publishing insight.

# Conventions

We attempted to preserve the integrity of original documents. Occasionally we added paragraphing for readability. For instance, we heavily paragraphed the Declaration of Independence (Lesson 16). The original is two paragraphs.[1]

In primary source Jefferson and Lincoln documents, if *The Papers of Thomas Jefferson*, *The Papers of Thomas Jefferson: Retirement Series*, or *The Collected Works of Abraham Lincoln* italicize words, we underline them (as Jefferson and Lincoln did in the handwritten originals). Brackets contain our text insertions that clarify a word or phrase. Bolded brackets contain existing insertions in cited quotations.

Spelling (including misspellings), grammar, letter case, abbreviations, archaic expressions, and Thomas Jefferson's frequent use of "it's" for "its," and "past" for "passed," are preserved in letters, speeches, and quotations. Frequently Jefferson did not begin sentences with capital letters. He generally put a period after a day of the month (for example, "May 26" is "May 26." even if in the middle of a sentence), or year (for example, "1813" is "1813." even if in the middle of a sentence). Jefferson frequently used two-digit values for years (for example, "1813" is "13." even if in the middle of a sentence).

# INTRODUCTION

*The Tyranny of Public Discourse* is an easier read if you initially set aside what you already know about rhetoric, logic, facts, reasoning, argument, persuasion, and demonstration. "Fine wine tastes best when poured into a clean and empty glass."[1]

Compositions of Thomas Jefferson and Abraham Lincoln light a road to the persuasive structure of the six elements of a proposition. Lincoln put the goal succinctly: "I do not seek applause, nor to amuse the people, I want to convince them."[2]

Abraham Lincoln used the logical structure of a six-element proposition to draft the Gettysburg Address.[3] Thomas Jefferson used the same structure to draft the American Declaration of Independence.[4] The elements are 1) **Enunciation** (contains a **given** and a **sought**); 2) **Exposition**; 3) **Specification**; 4) **Construction**; 5) **Proof**; and 6) **Conclusion**. Each element is a structural concept with a one-sentence definition. Proclus preserved the six one-sentence definitions.[5]

John Adams and Thomas Jefferson were members of the five-person Continental Congress committee appointed on June 11, 1776, to draft the American Declaration of Independence.[6] In an August 6, 1822, letter to Timothy Pickering, Adams unknowingly articulated the reason ("Reason third" below) to internalize the six elements of a proposition. The letter explained Adams' maneuver that resulted in Jefferson drafting the Declaration of Independence. Adams wrote, "Jefferson proposed to me to make the draught."

> Adams: I said, "I will not."
>
> Jefferson: "You should do it."
>
> Adams: "Oh! no."
>
> Jefferson: "Why will you not? You ought to do it."
>
> Adams: "I will not."
>
> Jefferson: "Why?"
>
> Adams: "Reasons enough."
>
> Jefferson: "What can be your reasons?"
>
> Adams: "Reason first—You are a Virginian, and a Virginian ought to appear at the head of this business. Reason second—I am obnoxious, suspected, and unpopular.

You are very much otherwise. Reason third—You can write ten times better than I can."[7]

To understand any one element, there must be at least a rudimentary grasp of all six. While the six elements can be listed linearly, they interact multidimensionally. Each element synergistically connects to the other five with simple elegance and textured complexity. The result is natural persuasion.

*The Tyranny of Public Discourse: Abraham Lincoln's Six-Element Antidote for Meaningful and Persuasive Writing* illuminates structured composition within the six elements of a proposition. The six-element method of composition embeds locational purpose into words. This is true whether leading a nation through a war with a Gettysburg Address (Lessons 1 through 6), advocating a revolution with a Declaration of Independence (Lesson 16), or just saying goodbye with a Farewell Address (Lesson 10). Internalizing the six elements for writing and speaking provides rewards: Critical thinking becomes automatic; listening is artful; persuasive composition is natural; and leadership sharpens.

Thomas Jefferson was among America's best educated individuals.[8] Abraham Lincoln's "defective" formal education was less than one year.[9] In the five years after Lincoln's single two-year Congressional term, Lincoln elevated his oratory. He set out to discover what it means to demonstrate.[10] Between 1849 and 1854, he figured it out through self-study of Euclid's first six books (plane geometry).[11] *The Tyranny of Public Discourse* is the guidebook Lincoln lacked.

How did the six elements hide so long? What were the consequences? Are you satisfied with today's public discourse? Do you think there should be a better way? Would you like a competitive edge?

Stephan A. Douglas questioned the integrity of U.S. Senator Lyman Trumbull concerning a Trumbull speech. In the fourth Lincoln-Douglas debate, September 18, 1858, Lincoln responded to the Douglas personal attack on Trumbull:

> Why, sir, there is not a word in Trumbull's speech that depends on Trumbull's veracity at all. He has only arrayed the evidence [the **Construction**] and told you what follows as a matter of reasoning [the **Proof**]. There is not a statement in the whole speech that depends on Trumbull's word. If you have ever studied geometry, you remember that by a course of reasoning Euclid proves that all the angles in a triangle are equal to two right angles. Euclid has shown you how to work it out. Now, if you undertake to disprove that proposition, and to show that it is erroneous, would you prove it to be false by calling Euclid a liar?[12]

In his autobiography, Thomas Jefferson hinted he used Euclid's six-element method to structure the Virginia Statute for Religious Freedom (Lesson 16); he stated he drafted the statute in the form of "a singular proposition."[13]

The best evidence of the structure of selected Jefferson and Lincoln writings is the writings themselves. The same is true of Euclid. Euclid did not expressly reveal the six-element structure of the geometric demonstrations he edited or assembled.

Proclus preserved Euclid's definitional structure in his commentary on Euclid:

> Every problem and every theorem that is furnished with all its parts should contain the following elements: an enunciation, an exposition, a specification, a construction, a proof, and a conclusion.[14]

A relatively simple proposition may have three elements. Proclus said:

> The most essential ones, and those which are always present, are enunciation, proof, and conclusion; for it is alike necessary to know in advance what is being sought, to prove it by middle terms, and to collect what has been proved. It is impossible that any of these three should be lacking; the other parts are often brought in but are often left out when they serve no need.[15]

For instance:

## TWO TIMES THREE

**Enunciation**: [**Given**] Multiplication of positive integers is a process of adding a positive integer to itself a certain number of times. [**Sought**] What is 2 x 3?

**Proof**: 2 + 2 = 4.
  4 + 2 = 6.
  Three twos added equals six.

**Conclusion**: Therefore 2 x 3 = 6.

A well constructed six-element proposition can convey textured beauty. Each element extends non-linear, synergistic sinews among the other elements. This enables structural beauty that is easy to feel, but hard to describe unless one understands the six elements. Six-element persuasive compositions are anchored and modulated by the logical location of words, phrases, and paragraphs. With locational structure embedded into language, scientific reasoning highlights weak arguments, and spotlights strong arguments. Words become easier, and expression more beautiful. Properly done, logic is iron, and persuasion is natural. Six elements light the path to reasoned persuasion.

Structural, synergistic binding among the elements makes them special. Memorize element names and order.

1. **Enunciation**
    a. **Given**
    b. **Sought**
2. **Exposition**
3. **Specification**
4. **Construction**
5. **Proof**
6. **Conclusion**

The ancient Greek philosopher Proclus wrote over a million words on multiple subjects.[16] Among those words are six sentences that define the six elements of a proposition. Read and re-read each definition. Become sensitive to the relationships they create.

**Enunciation:** "The **enunciation** states what is **given** and what is being **sought** from it."[17] The **Enunciation** answers the question: *Why are we here?*[18]

**Exposition:** "The **exposition** takes separately what is **given** and prepares it in advance for use in the investigation."[19] The **Exposition** answers the question: *What additional facts are needed to know what to investigate?*[20]

**Specification:** "The **specification** takes separately the thing that is **sought** and makes clear precisely what it is."[21] The **Specification** answers the question: *What must be demonstrated to resolve what is sought?*[22]

**Construction:** "The **construction** adds what is lacking in the **given** for finding what is **sought**."[23] The **Construction** answers the question: *How do the facts lead to what is sought?*[24]

**Proof:** "The **proof** draws the proposed inference by reasoning scientifically from the propositions that have been admitted."[25] The **Proof** answers the question: *How does the admitted truth confirm the proposed inference?*[26]

**Conclusion:** "The **conclusion** reverts to the **enunciation**, confirming what has been proved."[27] The **Conclusion** answers the question: *What was demonstrated?*[28]

The six elements of a proposition collectively define a demonstration. Picture a three-sided pyramid with the **Conclusion** at the top. In **Diagrams Introduction.1** and **Introduction.2** earth tone is factual foundation; green is logical direction; red is argument.

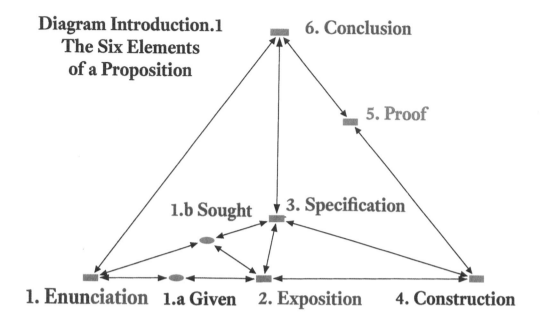

**Diagram Introduction.1**
**The Six Elements**
**of a Proposition**

6. Conclusion

5. Proof

1.b Sought     3. Specification

1. Enunciation     1.a Given     2. Exposition     4. Construction

**Diagram Introduction.2** presents the elements with Proclus definitions:

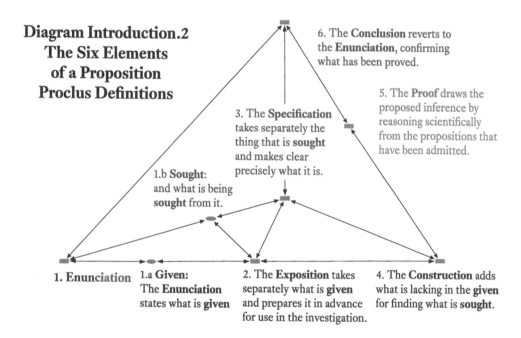

**Diagram Introduction.2**
**The Six Elements**
**of a Proposition**
**Proclus Definitions**

6. The **Conclusion** reverts to the **Enunciation**, confirming what has been proved.

5. The **Proof** draws the proposed inference by reasoning scientifically from the propositions that have been admitted.

3. The **Specification** takes separately the thing that is **sought** and makes clear precisely what it is.

1.b **Sought**: and what is being **sought** from it.

1. Enunciation     1.a **Given**: The **Enunciation** states what is **given**

2. The **Exposition** takes separately what is **given** and prepares it in advance for use in the investigation.

4. The **Construction** adds what is lacking in the **given** for finding what is **sought**.

Reasoned persuasion is built on facts. Persuasion requires credibility.

  a) To be credible, trust must be earned.
  b) To earn trust, one must be truthful.
  c) To be truthful, facts must be presented.
  d) Trust also requires civility, and respect for other viewpoints.
  e) Credibility increases when argument is withheld until late in the proposition (the fifth element).

An honest reputation must be cultivated. The goal is to convince. A six-element demonstration at the minimum must permit a listener or reader to make room for the possibility the proposition is valid.

Carefully framed propositions, with carefully timed argument (**Proof**) anchored in fact, are the basis of reasoned persuasion. A well-formed, scientifically reasoned argument does not require genius. It requires discipline, fact, and a well-investigated, well-framed, provable hypothesis (**Specification**).

Slavery and national survival were divisive issues that had to be confronted. Abraham Lincoln's speech composition sometimes began with randomly composed fragments, almost like notes on 3 x 5 cards. Lincoln's son Robert remembered Lincoln "was accustomed to make many scraps of notes or memoranda."[29] Abraham Lincoln's law partner, William Herndon, recalled Lincoln's composition of the House Divided speech:

> [H]e wrote that fine effort—an argumentative one, in slips—put those slips in his hat, numbering them, and when he was done with the ideas, he gathered up the scraps—put them in the right order, and wrote out his speech.[30]

Structure modulates timing and coalesces substance. Keep in mind:

  a) Facts;
  b) Civility, honesty, and credibility;
  c) The "geography" (location) of words; and
  d) Argument location (timing).

Writers usually know what their own words, sentences, and paragraphs mean. If the goal is to communicate just with oneself, most people write well. Writers must get outside of their skin to persuade others. That, not writing itself, makes writing difficult.

At some point, analyze every word, phrase, sentence, and paragraph from the viewpoint of each type of likely reader or listener. Determine whether there is any way to deliberately misconstrue any word, phrase, sentence, or paragraph. Look for a simple change to make it impossible to misconstrue.

Refine without fattening. Resist the temptation to add verbiage. Resist the temptation to say everything in a single sentence or paragraph. Beware of adjectives and adverbs. Useful at times, adjectives and adverbs are not a substitute for objective facts and tight reasoning. William Strunk, Jr., and E. B. White warned in *The Elements of Style,* "Write with nouns and verbs, not with adjectives and adverbs."[31] Initially keep language tight and terse.

Clear, concise language, good grammar, proper spelling, and good reputation, have little directly to do with the six elements of a proposition. But because credibility is everything regarding persuasion, anything that affects credibility is crucial. The Jefferson letters in this Introduction are about basic skills.

In 1808, President Thomas Jefferson wrote to his grandson Thomas Jefferson Randolph regarding concise summary:

> Dear Jefferson                                                    Washington Dec. 7. 08
> ...The difficulty you experience in abridging the lectures is not unexpected. I remember when I began a regular course of study. I determined to abridge in a common place book, every thing of value which I read. at first I could shorten it very little: but after a while I was able to put a page of a book into 2. or 3. sentences, without omitting any portion of the substance. go on therefore with courage & you will find it grow easier & easier. besides obligin you to understand the subject, & fixing it in your memory, it will learn you the most valuable art of condensing your thoughts & expressing them in the fewest words possible. no stile of writing is so delightful as that which is all pith, which never omits a necessary word, nor uses an unnecessary one. the finest models of this existing are Sallust and Tacitus, which on that account are worthy of constant study. and that you may have every just encouragement I will add that from what I observe of the natural stile of your letters I think you will readily attain this kind of perfection...
>
> Th. Jefferson[32]

Thomas Jefferson discussed plain English regarding a Virginia public education statute he drafted. Jefferson wrote to Joseph C. Cabell in 1817:

> Dear Sir                                                    Poplar Forest. Sep. 9. 17.
> I promised you that I would put into the form of a bill my plan of establishing the elementary schools, without taking a cent from the literary fund. I have had leisure at this place to do this, & now send you the result.

if 12. or 1500. schools are to be placed under one general administration, an attention so divided will amount to a dereliction of them to themselves. it is surely better then to place each school at once under the care of those most interested in it's conduct. in this way the literary fund is left untouched to compleat at once the whole system of education, by establishing a college in every district of about 80. miles square, for the 2d grade of education, to wit, languages antient and modern, and for the 3d grade a single university, in which the sciences shall be taught in their highest degree.

I should apologise perhaps for the style of this bill. I dislike the verbose & intricate style of the modern English statutes, and in our revised code I endeavored to restore it to the simple one of the antient statutes, in such original bills as I drew in that work. I suppose the reformation has not been acceptable, as it has been little followed. you however can easily correct this bill to the taste of my brother lawyers, by making every other word a 'said' or 'aforesaid,' and saying every thing over 2. or 3. times, so as that nobody but we of the craft can untwist the diction, and find out what it means; and that too not so plainly but that we may conscientiously divide, one half on each side.

mend it therefore in form and substance to the orthodox taste, & make it what it should be; or, if you think it radically wrong, try something else, & let us make a beginning in some way. no matter how wrong; experience will amend it as we go along, and make it effectual in the end.

I shall see you of course at our stated Visitation, and hope all the gentlemen will consider Monticello as the rendezvous of the preceding day or evening. I salute you with friendship and respect.

Th. Jefferson[33]

Vermonter Horatio G. Spafford was a geographer, inventor, and editor.[34] Spafford's February 28, 1822, letter to Thomas Jefferson discussed Spafford's planned spelling book:

I copy, on the other sides, its title-page, & beg of thee to favor me with thy views. Canst thou suggest any improvement? I hope I shall be able to have thy examination of a printed copy. Until it is published, I do not want a knowledge of it to get out.[35]

Jefferson replied:

Dear Sir                                    Monticello Mar. 19. 22.
I duly recieved your favor of Feb. 28. and take a friendly interest in the good and the evil which you, as all our human brethren, have to encounter in the path of life. I hope your literary labors will prove advantageous to yourself and useful to the world. the occupation of the mind is surely that which brings most happiness.

but with respect to your Apprentice's Spelling book, you could not have appealed to a more incompetent judge than myself. I have never in my life had occasion to attend to that elementary stage of education, nor to reflect at all on the different methods of conducting it to best advantage. this is a solid reason for my not undertaking to give an opinion on it, added to another which I have been obliged to lay down as a law to myself, of not usurping the right of saying to the public what is worthy or not worthy of their attention. this is the office of Critics by profession in whose line I am the least practised of all men living. with my regrets therefore that I can offer nothing but my best wishes for the success of all your literary and other labors, accept the assurance of my esteem & respect.

Th. Jefferson[36]

The purpose of persuasive writing is demonstration to others. Demonstration requires thorough knowledge of the issues, the facts, and the audience. A six-element demonstration puts its writer in a teaching role. Teaching usually begins with a process of presenting agreed facts and agreed ideas. A persuasive demonstration, or a process of agreed propositions, should respectfully teach in order to convince, or to advance knowledge.

Language is expression; structure is place. Language offers a system for using words; structure offers a method for using language.

Demarcation exercises in *The Tyranny of Public Discourse* include writings and speeches of Thomas Jefferson, Abraham Lincoln, and others.[37] Exercises, hints, and suggested solutions are in Lessons 9, 10, 17, 18, and 19.

Questions at the end of lessons focus discussion, develop composition insight, and enhance persuasive ability. It can be beneficial to read the questions, and loosely keep them in mind. A thoughtful, written answer is more beneficial. A six-element essay in response to a question may be best.

A major goal of *The Tyranny of Public Discourse* is to internalize the six-element composition method for persuasive demonstrations. *The Tyranny of Public Discourse* includes composition strategies in Lessons 12, 13, 14, and 15. Critical thinking is just as important as the elements. Fortunately, critical thinking is a natural by-product of internalizing the six elements.

Thomas Jefferson commented to John Adams on October 14, 1816, regarding Antoine Louis Destutt de Tracy's treatise on political economy, "…all it's principles are demonstrated with the severity of Euclid, and, like him, without ever using a superfluous word."[38] Jefferson edited William Duane's French-to-English translation of Destutt de Tracy's *A Treatise on Political*

*Economy*.[39] Jefferson commented in an October 1818 letter to Destutt de Tracy's publisher Joseph Milligan:

> it would be difficult to do justice, in any translation, to the style of the original, in which no word is unnecessary, no word can be changed for the better, and severity of logic results in that brevity, to which we wish all science reduced.[40]

In 1938, Stuart Chase wrote in *The Tyranny of Words*:

> I have written several books and many articles, but only lately have I begun to inquire into the nature of the tools I use. This is a curious oversight when one stops to consider it. Carpenters, masons, and engineers who give no thought to their tools and instruments are not likely to erect very durable structures.[41]

Chase described communication disconnects, but stopped short of a specific solution. He discussed Euclid and plane geometry. He "saw" Euclid's geometric substance (geometry), but did not "see" Euclid's method (the six elements). Chase understood Euclid's geometry and its mathematical limitations.[42] He did not "see" the six elements, and the elements' unlimited structural power as vessels for words.[43]

Chase's eyes were on the bark of the tree; the forest was invisible. Chase missed Euclid's linguistic use of the scientific method. Near the end of his almost 400-page book, Chase keenly reasoned, "We desperately need a language structure for the clear communication of observations, deductions, and ideas concerning the environment in which we live today."[44]

After a list and discussion of communication breakdowns,[45] Chase articulated an appealing general solution:

> The age-old disagreements in these studies [relating to language disconnects] will continue until, as [Lancelot] Hogben [author of *Mathematics for the Million*] says, "we make the language of science part of the language of mankind, and realize that the future of human reason lies with those who are prepared to face the task of rationally planning the instruments of communication."[46]

That *is* the solution. And that is what the six-element "instruments of communication" of Thomas Jefferson and Abraham Lincoln teach. Their six-element writings reveal a rational, structural solution. It is a "language of science" for human issues.

## BROWN, GREEN, AND RED BUILDING BLOCKS

**Enunciation**: [**Given**] Brown earth is foundation. Green is logic that flows from a firm foundation. Red is carefully modulated argument with pinpoint location.

[**Sought**] Proper foundation and directional logic pushed through the fire of argument, lead to a firm, living **Conclusion**.

**Exposition**: The six elements of a proposition can be grouped into three categories: Factual Development (brown), Logical Progression (green), and Argument (red).

**Specification**: Each of the three categories of the six elements of a proposition is critical. Argument is the most delicate.

**Construction**: Argument under control is properly positioned, and perfectly timed for persuasive punch.

**Proof**: Facts are the most important building blocks of a proposition because they are the basis of credibility. Facts require direction to nurture logical development. Properly timed argument sustains a six-element proposition. Logic fertilizes fact. The six elements combine to stimulate growth.

**Conclusion**: Argument confined to a proper place, the fifth element (**Proof**), with the proper tone, nurtures a living proposition with factual foundation and logical strength. The **Conclusion** confirms what was demonstrated.

## QUESTIONS

ONE: Why is language important?

TWO: What does agreement have to do with language?

THREE: What would be the effect on conversation if no two people used a common language?

FOUR: How does agreement lead to persuasion?

FIVE: Is there a tension between agreement and creativity? If so, what is the tension and why does it exist?

SIX: What is the definition of good writing?

SEVEN: Why is persuasive writing difficult?

EIGHT: What is the difference between language and structure?

NINE: What is the relationship between persuasion and language?

TEN: How is language used to persuade?

ELEVEN: How is language best used to persuade?

# LESSON ONE: THE FIRST ELEMENT

# ENUNCIATION: WHY ARE WE HERE?

The **Enunciation** is the first of the six elements of a proposition.

**Proclus definition:** "The **enunciation** states what is *given* and what is being *sought* from it."[1]

### Address Delivered at the Dedication of the Cemetery at Gettysburg
### President Abraham Lincoln[2]
November 19, 1863

1. Four score and seven years ago our fathers brought forth on this continent, a new nation, conceived in Liberty, and dedicated to the proposition that all men are created equal.

Now we are engaged in a great civil war, testing whether that nation, or any nation so conceived and so dedicated, can long endure.

We are met on a great battle-field of that war. We have come to dedicate a portion of that field, as a final resting place for those who here gave their lives that that nation might live. It is altogether fitting and proper that we should do this.

But, in a larger sense, we can not dedicate—we can not consecrate—we can not hallow—this ground. The brave men, living and dead, who struggled here, have consecrated it, far above our poor power to add or detract. The world will little note, nor long remember what we say here, but it can never forget what they did here. It is for us the living, rather, to be dedicated here to the unfinished work which they who fought here have thus far so nobly advanced. It is rather for us to be here dedicated to the great task remaining before us—that from these honored dead we take increased devotion to that cause for which they gave the last full measure of devotion—that we here highly resolve that these dead shall not have died in vain—that this nation, under God, shall have a new birth of freedom—and that government of the people, by the people, for the people, shall not perish from the earth.

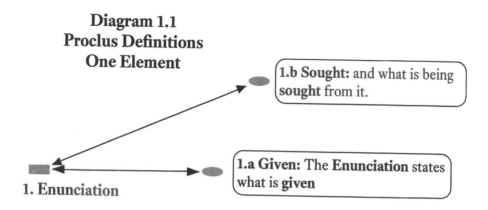

**Diagram 1.1**
**Proclus Definitions**
**One Element**

**1.b Sought:** and what is being **sought** from it.

**1.a Given:** The **Enunciation** states what is **given**

**1. Enunciation**

The **Enunciation** answers the question: *Why are we here?*

**Function:**

*Given:* Indisputable facts framed the problem. The country was founded in 1776. The Civil War was ongoing.

*Sought*: A high-level, neutrally framed issue was drafted as a pass or fail test. The *sought* questioned whether a nation "so conceived and so dedicated" can long endure. The *sought* generally circumscribed the outer limits of the Investigation (Lesson 11).

Credibility started in the **Enunciation** with the *given* and *sought*, and built element by element to the **Proof** (Lesson 5-argument). It was capped by the **Conclusion** (Lesson 6).

Each element enforced timing. Location disciplines language. The six elements are timing's framework.

**Tone:** A *given* should be self-evident, base-level facts. The *sought* should be a fairly neutral, and a somewhat general identification of the issue.

**ENUNCIATION:** [**Given**] Four score and seven years ago our fathers brought forth on this continent, a new nation, conceived in Liberty, and dedicated to the proposition that all men are created equal. Now we are engaged in a great civil war, [**Sought**] testing whether that nation, or any nation so conceived and so dedicated, can long endure.

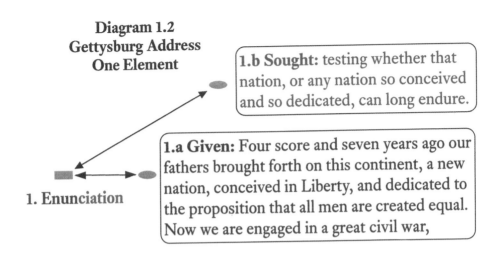

**Diagram 1.2
Gettysburg Address
One Element**

**1.b Sought:** testing whether that nation, or any nation so conceived and so dedicated, can long endure.

**1.a Given:** Four score and seven years ago our fathers brought forth on this continent, a new nation, conceived in Liberty, and dedicated to the proposition that all men are created equal. Now we are engaged in a great civil war,

**1. Enunciation**

## THOMAS JEFFERSON TO JOHN STOCKDALE, FEBRUARY 1, 1787

From Paris, United States Minister to France Thomas Jefferson wrote London publisher and bookseller John Stockdale regarding publication of Jefferson's *Notes on the State of Virginia*.[3] The **given** described Jefferson's resistance to previous attempts to publish the notes on Virginia. The **sought** identified Jefferson's changed view: to publish. The six-element letter will demonstrate how to accomplish publication.

> **Enunciation:** [**Given**] You have two or three times proposed to me the printing my Notes on Virginia. I never did intend to have them made public, because they are little interesting to the rest of the world. [**Sought**] But as a translation of them is coming out, I have concluded to let the original appear also.

## THOMAS JEFFERSON TO HENRY DEARBORN
### FEBRUARY 18, 1801

In a February 18, 1801, letter to Henry Dearborn, President-Elect Thomas Jefferson sought a Secretary of War.[4] The **given** set up Jefferson's proposition with a creative term for the office of President: "chair of the US." Jefferson's **sought** was to find qualified public servants.

> **Enunciation:** [**Given**] The House of Representatives having yesterday concluded their choice of a person for the chair of the US. and called me to

that office, [**Sought**] it now becomes necessary to provide an administration composed of persons whose qualifications and standing have possessed them of the public confidence, and whose wisdom may ensure to our fellow citizens the advantages they sanguinely expect.

## THOMAS JEFFERSON TO MARY JEFFERSON EPPES MARCH 3, 1802

Mary Jefferson Eppes was one of President Jefferson's two daughters.[5] The **given** in the March 3, 1802, letter to Mary contained facts related to Jefferson's desire to see her. The **sought** was a visit from his daughter.

> **Enunciation:** [**Given**] I observed to you some time ago that during the session of Congress I should be able to write to you but seldom; and so it has turned out. your's of Jan. 24. I recieved in due time, after which mr Eppes's letters of Feb. 1. & 2. confirmed to me the news, always welcome, of your's & Francis's health. since this I have no news of you. I see with great concern that I am not to have the pleasure of meeting you in Albemarle in the spring. [**Sought**] I had entertained the hope mr Eppes & yourself would have past the summer there. and being there, that the two families could have come together on a visit here. I observe your reluctance at the idea of that visit, but for your own happiness must advise you to get the better of it.

## THOMAS JEFFERSON TO TUNIS WORTMAN, AUGUST 15, 1813

Former President Thomas Jefferson responded to New Yorker Tunis Wortman's request that Jefferson subscribe to Wortman's new newspaper.[6] The **given** confirmed Jefferson's subscription to the newspaper. The **sought** was only a one-year subscription.

> **Enunciation:** [**Given**] I return your subscription paper with my name willingly placed on it. [**Sought**] I have said <u>for one year</u>, and inclose the price, because I find myself happier in other branches of reading, than of newspapers.

## ABRAHAM LINCOLN TO GEORGE ROBERTSON, AUGUST 15, 1855

On July 9, 1855, Kentucky Judge George Robertson delivered an inscribed book he wrote, *Scrap Book on Law and Politics, Men and Times*. He left it in Springfield for Abraham Lincoln. Lincoln later wrote Robertson.[7] Lincoln's **given** was factual background about Robertson, the autographed book, the Missouri Compromise, and slavery. The **sought** suggested there will be no peaceful extinction of slavery.

> **Enunciation:** [**Given**] My dear Sir: The volume you left for me has been received. I am really grateful for the honor of your kind remembrance, as well as for the book. The partial reading I have already given it, has afforded me much of both pleasure and instruction. It was new to me that the exact question which led to the Missouri compromise, had arisen before it arose in regard to Missouri; and that you had taken so prominent a part in it. Your short, but able and patriotic speech upon that occasion, has not been improved upon since, by those holding the same views; and, with all the lights you then had, the views you took appear to me as very reasonable.
>
> You are not a friend of slavery in the abstract. In that speech you spoke of "the peaceful extinction of slavery" and used other expressions indicating your belief that the thing was, at some time, to have an end[.] Since then we have had thirty six years of experience; [**Sought**] and this experience has demonstrated, I think, that there is no peaceful extinction of slavery in prospect for us.

## ABRAHAM LINCOLN TO SAMUEL C. DAVIS AND COMPANY
## NOVEMBER 17, 1858

Attorney Abraham Lincoln wrote this 1858 letter to fire a client.[8] The **given** briefly described what happened. The **sought** was to try to explain Lincoln's action or inaction.

> **Enunciation:** [**Given**] You perhaps need not to be reminded how I have been personally engaged the last three or four months. Your letter to Lincoln & Herndon, of Oct. 1st. complaining that the lands of those against whom we obtained judgments last winter for you, have not been sold on execution has just been handed to me to-day. [**Sought**] I will try to "explain how our" (your) "interests have been so much neglected" as you choose to express it.

## ABRAHAM LINCOLN TO DAVID HUNTER, OCTOBER 24, 1861

President Abraham Lincoln wrote General David Hunter shortly before Hunter's official appointment as Commander of the Western Department of the United States Army.[9] Hunter's assumption of command was the **given**. More was not necessary in the **given**. A unique **sought** for a Commander in Chief began, "I propose to offer you a few <u>suggestions</u>…"

> **Enunciation:** [**Given**] Sir: The command of the Department of the West having devolved upon you, [**Sought**] I propose to offer you a few <u>suggestions</u>, knowing how hazzardous it is to bind down a distant commander in the field to specific lines and operations, as so much always depends on a knowledge of localities & passing events. It is intended therefore, to leave a considerable margin for the exercise of your judgment & discretion.

## EUCLID'S PROPOSITION 1

Euclid used the six elements to structure plane geometry propositions. Proposition 1 carefully placed words within six-element structural vessels.[10]

> **Enunciation:** [**Given**] On a given finite straight line [**Sought**] to construct an equilateral triangle.[11]

## QUESTIONS

ONE: What is the best **Enunciation** among the Jefferson letters, Lincoln letters, and Proposition 1, in this lesson? Why?

TWO: How are a **given** and **sought** different from other ways to begin a speech, a letter, a story, or a joke?

THREE: How would you characterize the differences between the tone of a Jefferson **sought** and a Lincoln **sought**?

# Lesson Two: The Second Element

# Exposition: What Needs to be Investigated?

The **Exposition** is the second of the six elements.

**Proclus definition:** "The **exposition** takes separately what is *given* and prepares it in advance for use in the investigation."[1]

### Address Delivered at the Dedication of the Cemetery at Gettysburg[2]
November 19, 1863

1. Four score and seven years ago our fathers brought forth on this continent, a new nation, conceived in Liberty, and dedicated to the proposition that all men are created equal.

Now we are engaged in a great civil war, testing whether that nation, or any nation so conceived and so dedicated, can long endure. 2. We are met on a great battle-field of that war.

We have come to dedicate a portion of that field, as a final resting place for those who here gave their lives that that nation might live. It is altogether fitting and proper that we should do this.

But, in a larger sense, we can not dedicate—we can not consecrate—we can not hallow—this ground. The brave men, living and dead, who struggled here, have consecrated it, far above our poor power to add or detract. The world will little note, nor long remember what we say here, but it can never forget what they did here. It is for us the living, rather, to be dedicated here to the unfinished work which they who fought here have thus far so nobly advanced. It is rather for us to be here dedicated to the great task remaining before us—that from these honored dead we take increased devotion to that cause for which they gave the last full measure of devotion—that we here highly resolve that these dead shall not have died in vain—that this nation, under God, shall have a new birth of freedom—and that government of the people, by the people, for the people, shall not perish from the earth.

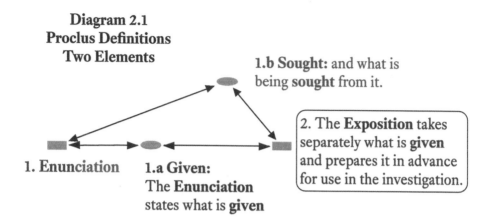

**Diagram 2.1**
**Proclus Definitions**
**Two Elements**

**1.b Sought:** and what is being **sought** from it.

1. Enunciation

**1.a Given:**
The **Enunciation** states what is **given**

2. The **Exposition** takes separately what is **given** and prepares it in advance for use in the investigation.

The **Exposition** answers the question: *What additional facts are needed to know what to investigate?*

**Function:** Factual development to enable the Investigation. The **Exposition** builds from the **Enunciation**.

Lincoln's **Exposition** added location: the Gettysburg Civil War battlefield. The **Exposition** leads to enough additional facts to form a hypothesis. The hypothesis is the **Specification's** proposed inference. An Investigation also leads to facts arrayed in the **Construction**.

**Tone:** Impartial, reasonably terse, instantly believable.

> **Enunciation:** [**Given**] Four score and seven years ago our fathers brought forth on this continent, a new nation, conceived in Liberty, and dedicated to the proposition that all men are created equal. Now we are engaged in a great civil war, [**Sought**] testing whether that nation, or any nation so conceived and so dedicated, can long endure.
>
> **EXPOSITION:** We are met on a great battle-field of that war.

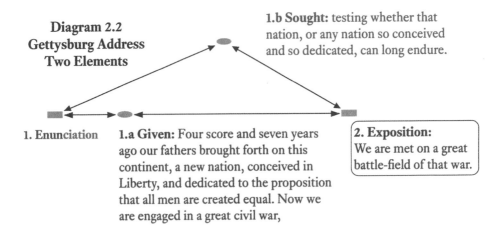

**Diagram 2.2
Gettysburg Address
Two Elements**

**1.b Sought:** testing whether that nation, or any nation so conceived and so dedicated, can long endure.

1. Enunciation

**1.a Given:** Four score and seven years ago our fathers brought forth on this continent, a new nation, conceived in Liberty, and dedicated to the proposition that all men are created equal. Now we are engaged in a great civil war,

**2. Exposition:**
We are met on a great battle-field of that war.

The **Exposition** was factual and necessary for the Investigation.

Before leaving Springfield for Washington on February 11, 1861, President-Elect Abraham Lincoln gave a short farewell address (Lesson 10). The **given** recited Lincoln's sadness to depart Springfield. The **Exposition** built factually:

> To this place, and the kindness of these people, I owe every thing. Here I have lived a quarter of a century, and have passed from a young to an old man. Here my children have been born, and one is buried.

The tone was set for a farewell that moved from sentimental observations to national issues.

In the Declaration of Independence (Lesson 16), the **Exposition** presented facts necessary to conduct an Investigation. The Investigation refined and transformed the more general **sought** to a precise **Specification**. The Investigation made way for discovery of grievances marshaled into a long **Construction**. The Declaration's **Exposition**:

> We hold these truths to be self-evident, that all men are created equal, that they are endowed by their Creator with certain unalienable Rights, that among these are Life, Liberty and the pursuit of Happiness. That to secure these rights, Governments are instituted among Men, deriving their just powers from the consent of the governed, That whenever any Form of Government becomes destructive of these ends, it is the Right of the People to alter or to abolish it, and to institute new Government, laying its foundation on such principles and organizing its powers in such form, as to them shall seem most likely to effect their Safety and Happiness. Prudence, indeed, will dictate that Governments long established should not be changed for light and transient causes; and accordingly all experience hath shewn, that mankind are more disposed to suffer, while evils

are sufferable, than to right themselves by abolishing the forms to which they are accustomed.

## THOMAS JEFFERSON TO JOHN STOCKDALE, FEBRUARY 1, 1787

The goal of this Thomas Jefferson proposition was to resolve whether John Stockdale would publish Jefferson's *Notes on the State of Virginia*. The **Exposition** contained additional facts regarding publication.

> **Enunciation:** [**Given**] You have two or three times proposed to me the printing my Notes on Virginia. I never did intend to have them made public, because they are little interesting to the rest of the world. [**Sought**] But as a translation of them is coming out, I have concluded to let the original appear also.

> **Exposition:** I have therefore corrected a copy, and made some additions. I have moreover had a map engraved, which is worth more than the book.

## THOMAS JEFFERSON TO HENRY DEARBORN
## FEBRUARY 18, 1801

The **Exposition** contained a basis for Henry Dearborn to become leader of the Department of War.

> **Enunciation:** [**Given**] The House of Representatives having yesterday concluded their choice of a person for the chair of the US. and called me to that office, [**Sought**] it now becomes necessary to provide an administration composed of persons whose qualifications and standing have possessed them of the public confidence, and whose wisdom may ensure to our fellow citizens the advantages they sanguinely expect.

> **Exposition:** on a review of the characters in the different states proper for the different departments, I have had no hesitation in considering you as the person to whom it would be most advantageous to the public to confide the Department of war.

## THOMAS JEFFERSON TO MARY JEFFERSON EPPES
## MARCH 3, 1802

The **Exposition** stated President Jefferson's concern that his daughter tended to isolate herself. This important fact built the proposition.

> **Enunciation:** [**Given**] I observed to you some time ago that during the session of Congress I should be able to write to you but seldom; and so it has turned out. your's of Jan. 24. I recieved in due time, after which mr Eppes's letters of Feb. 1. & 2. confirmed to me the news, always welcome, of your's & Francis's health. since this I have no news of you. I see with great concern that I am not to have the pleasure of meeting you in Albemarle in the spring. [**Sought**] I had entertained the hope mr Eppes & yourself would have past the summer there. and being there, that the two families could have come together on a visit here. I observe your reluctance at the idea of that visit, but for your own happiness must advise you to get the better of it.

> **Exposition:** I think I discover in you a willingness to withdraw from society more than is prudent.

## THOMAS JEFFERSON TO TUNIS WORTMAN, AUGUST 15, 1813

The **Exposition** presented facts regarding Thomas Jefferson's newspaper reading habits. The **Exposition's** reference to Wortman's "case" was needed to move from the **sought** to a more precise **Specification**.

> **Enunciation:** [**Given**] I return your subscription paper with my name willingly placed on it. [**Sought**] I have said <u>for one year</u>, and inclose the price, because I find myself happier in other branches of reading, than of newspapers.

> **Exposition:** I read 2. or 3. a week of the old ones still, but engage for no new ones; and have done it in your case, because I am confident it will be conducted in a good spirit,

## ABRAHAM LINCOLN TO GEORGE ROBERTSON, AUGUST 15, 1855

The **Exposition** highlighted the failure to effect gradual emancipation. It gave the example of Kentucky.

> **Enunciation: [Given]** My dear Sir: The volume you left for me has been received. I am really grateful for the honor of your kind remembrance, as well as for the book. The partial reading I have already given it, has afforded me much of both pleasure and instruction. It was new to me that the exact question which led to the Missouri compromise, had arisen before it arose in regard to Missouri; and that you had taken so prominent a part in it. Your short, but able and patriotic speech upon that occasion, has not been improved upon since, by those holding the same views; and, with all the lights you then had, the views you took appear to me as very reasonable.

> You are not a friend of slavery in the abstract. In that speech you spoke of "the peaceful extinction of slavery" and used other expressions indicating your belief that the thing was, at some time, to have an end[.] Since then we have had thirty six years of experience; **[Sought]** and this experience has demonstrated, I think, that there is no peaceful extinction of slavery in prospect for us.

> **Exposition:** The signal failure of Henry Clay, and other good and great men, in 1849, to effect any thing in favor of gradual emancipation in Kentucky, together with a thousand other signs, extinguishes that hope utterly.

## ABRAHAM LINCOLN TO SAMUEL C. DAVIS AND COMPANY
## NOVEMBER 17, 1858

The **Exposition** described Lincoln's effort for his client. It concluded: "My mind is made up". The **Exposition's** facts set up the resolution.

> **Enunciation: [Given]** You perhaps need not to be reminded how I have been personally engaged the last three or four months. Your letter to Lincoln & Herndon, of Oct. 1st. complaining that the lands of those against whom we obtained judgments last winter for you, have not been sold on execution has just been handed to me to-day. **[Sought]** I will try to "explain how our" (your) "interests have been so much neglected" as you choose to express it.

**Exposition:** After these judgments were obtained we wrote you that under our law, the selling of land on execution is a delicate and dangerous, matter; that it could not be done safely, without a careful examination of titles; and also of the <u>value</u> of the property. Our letters to you will show this. To do this would require a canvass of half the State. We were puzzled, & you sent no definite instructions. At length we employed a young man to visit all the localities, and make as accurate a report on titles and values as he could. He did this, expending three or four weeks time, and as he said, over a hundred dollars of his own money in doing so. When this was done we wrote you, asking if we should sell and bid in for you in accordance with this information. This letter you never answered. My mind is made up.

## ABRAHAM LINCOLN TO DAVID HUNTER, OCTOBER 24, 1861

The **Exposition** described the likely location of the rebel army, information necessary for Investigation of what was to be resolved.

**Enunciation:** [**Given**] Sir: The command of the Department of the West having devolved upon you, [**Sought**] I propose to offer you a few <u>suggestions</u>, knowing how hazzardous it is to bind down a distant commander in the field to specific lines and operations, as so much always depends on a knowledge of localities & passing events. It is intended therefore, to leave a considerable margin for the exercise of your judgment & discretion.

**Exposition:** The main rebel army (Prices) west of the Mississippi, is believed to have passed Dade county, in full retreat upon North-Western Arkansas, leaving Missouri almost freed from the enemy, excepting in the South-East of the State.

## EUCLID'S PROPOSITION 1

Euclid's Proposition 1 contained an easy to understand **Exposition**:

**Enunciation:** [**Given**] On a given finite straight line [**Sought**] to construct an equilateral triangle.

**Exposition:** Let AB be the given finite straight line.

A————————————B

## QUESTIONS

ONE: What is the best **Exposition** in this lesson? Why?

TWO: What is the difference between a fact and an opinion?

THREE: How are facts in an **Exposition** different from facts in a **given**?

FOUR: Which **Exposition** in this lesson best frames the Investigation? How?

FIVE: What is the purpose of an Investigation?

SIX: What is the definition of an Investigation? How does it work? Why does it work?

# SPECIFICATION: THE HYPOTHESIS

The **Specification** is the third of the six elements.

**Proclus definition:** "The **specification** takes separately the thing that is *sought* and makes clear precisely what it is."[1]

### Address Delivered at the Dedication of the Cemetery at Gettysburg[2]
#### November 19, 1863

1. Four score and seven years ago our fathers brought forth on this continent, a new nation, conceived in Liberty, and dedicated to the proposition that all men are created equal.

Now we are engaged in a great civil war, testing whether that nation, or any nation so conceived and so dedicated, can long endure. 2. We are met on a great battlefield of that war. 3. We have come to dedicate a portion of that field, as a final resting place for those who here gave their lives that that nation might live. It is altogether fitting and proper that we should do this.

But, in a larger sense, we can not dedicate—we can not consecrate—we can not hallow—this ground. The brave men, living and dead, who struggled here, have consecrated it, far above our poor power to add or detract. The world will little note, nor long remember what we say here, but it can never forget what they did here. It is for us the living, rather, to be dedicated here to the unfinished work which they who fought here have thus far so nobly advanced. It is rather for us to be here dedicated to the great task remaining before us—that from these honored dead we take increased devotion to that cause for which they gave the last full measure of devotion—that we here highly resolve that these dead shall not have died in vain—that this nation, under God, shall have a new birth of freedom—and that government of the people, by the people, for the people, shall not perish from the earth.

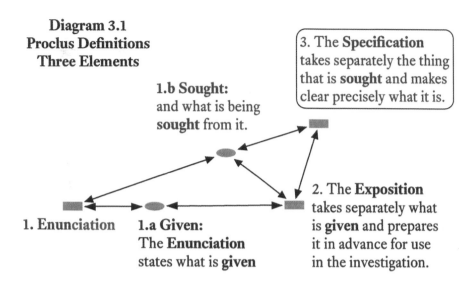

**Diagram 3.1**
**Proclus Definitions**
**Three Elements**

**1.b Sought:**
and what is being
**sought** from it.

3. The **Specification**
takes separately the thing
that is **sought** and makes
clear precisely what it is.

1. Enunciation        **1.a Given:**
The **Enunciation**
states what is **given**

2. The **Exposition**
takes separately what
is **given** and prepares
it in advance for use
in the investigation.

The **Specification** answers the question: *What must be demonstrated to resolve what is sought?*

**Function:** Framed by indisputable facts in the *given*, and additional facts in the **Exposition**, the high-level, neutral *sought* (testing survival of a nation so conceived) is focused in the **Specification**: They, "gave their lives that that nation might live". That proposed inference resulted from the Investigation.

**Tone:** Not neutral. Not overstated. Scientific reasoning must be able to confirm the **Specification's** hypothesis.

> **Enunciation:** [**Given**] Four score and seven years ago our fathers brought forth on this continent, a new nation, conceived in Liberty, and dedicated to the proposition that all men are created equal. Now we are engaged in a great civil war, [**Sought**] testing whether that nation, or any nation so conceived and so dedicated, can long endure.

> **Exposition:** We are met on a great battle-field of that war.

> **SPECIFICATION:** We have come to dedicate a portion of that field, as a final resting place for those who here gave their lives that that nation might live.  It is altogether fitting and proper that we should do this.

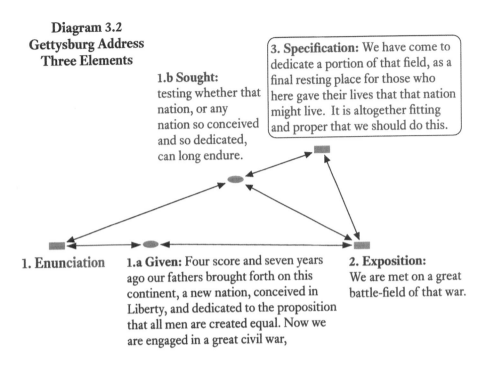

**Diagram 3.2**
**Gettysburg Address**
**Three Elements**

**3. Specification:** We have come to dedicate a portion of that field, as a final resting place for those who here gave their lives that that nation might live. It is altogether fitting and proper that we should do this.

**1.b Sought:** testing whether that nation, or any nation so conceived and so dedicated, can long endure.

**1. Enunciation**

**1.a Given:** Four score and seven years ago our fathers brought forth on this continent, a new nation, conceived in Liberty, and dedicated to the proposition that all men are created equal. Now we are engaged in a great civil war,

**2. Exposition:** We are met on a great battle-field of that war.

The Gettysburg Address was built on a few general facts: the founding of the United States, the Civil War, a battlefield location, and the dedication of a cemetery.

**Sought:** "testing whether that nation, or any nation so conceived and so dedicated, can long endure." The **sought** is neutral and general.

**Specification:** "We have come to dedicate a portion of that field, as a final resting place for those who here gave their lives that that nation might live. It is altogether fitting and proper that we should do this."

The **sought**, "testing", was clean and clear. It was on a high level that was more general and more neutral than the **Specification**. The **Specification** implied the nation must pass the test.

On March 4, 1865, President Lincoln delivered his Second Inaugural Address (Lesson 16). A high-level, impartial **sought** recited: "With high hope for the future, no prediction in regard to it is ventured." The **Exposition's** first paragraph ended with the sentence, "And the war came." This plain statement said what was necessary. The remainder of the **Exposition** described the war's circumstances and objectives. It presented the expectations of each side. The **Specification** focused: "Each looked for an easier triumph, and a result less fundamental and astounding." A compassionate and pragmatic base for the country's future was set. Leadership moved a skeptical audience.

The Declaration of Independence **sought** (Lesson 16) said, "they should declare the causes which impel them to the separation." The Declaration's fairly specific **sought** was more general than its biting **Specification**:

> But when a long train of abuses and usurpations, pursuing invariably the same Object evinces a design to reduce them under absolute Despotism, it is their right, it is their duty, to throw off such Government, and to provide new Guards for their future security. Such has been the patient sufferance of these Colonies; and such is now the necessity which constrains them to alter their former Systems of Government.

## THOMAS JEFFERSON TO JOHN STOCKDALE, FEBRUARY 1, 1787

The **Specification** recited precisely what would happen if Stockdale chose to print Jefferson's book.

**Enunciation:** [**Given**] You have two or three times proposed to me the printing my Notes on Virginia. I never did intend to have them made public, because they are little interesting to the rest of the world. [**Sought**] But as a translation of them is coming out, I have concluded to let the original appear also.

**Exposition:** I have therefore corrected a copy, and made some additions. I have moreover had a map engraved, which is worth more than the book.

**Specification:** If you chuse to print the work I will send you the corrected copy, and when it shall be nearly printed I will send the plate of the map.

## THOMAS JEFFERSON TO HENRY DEARBORN
## FEBRUARY 18, 1801

In the form of a question, the **Specification** expressed Thomas Jefferson's desire that Henry Dearborn become Secretary of War.

**Enunciation:** [**Given**] The House of Representatives having yesterday concluded their choice of a person for the chair of the US. and called me to that office, [**Sought**] it now becomes necessary to provide an administration composed of persons whose qualifications and standing have possessed them of the public confidence, and whose wisdom may ensure to our fellow citizens the advantages they sanguinely expect.

**Exposition:** on a review of the characters in the different states proper for the different departments, I have had no hesitation in considering you as the person to whom it would be most advantageous to the public to confide the Department of war.

**Specification:** may I therefore hope, Sir, that you will give your country the aid of your talents as Secretary of war?

## THOMAS JEFFERSON TO MARY JEFFERSON EPPES
## MARCH 3, 1802

The **Specification** presented the hypothesis that people should not isolate themselves. They should mix with the world.

**Enunciation:** [**Given**] I observed to you some time ago that during the session of Congress I should be able to write to you but seldom; and so it has turned out. your's of Jan. 24. I recieved in due time, after which mr Eppes's letters of Feb. 1. & 2. confirmed to me the news, always welcome, of your's & Francis's health. since this I have no news of you. I see with great concern that I am not to have the pleasure of meeting you in Albemarle in the spring. [**Sought**] I had entertained the hope mr Eppes & yourself would have past the summer there. and being there, that the two families could have come together on a visit here. I observe your reluctance at the idea of that visit, but for your own happiness must advise you to get the better of it.

**Exposition:** I think I discover in you a willingness to withdraw from society more than is prudent.

**Specification:** I am convinced our own happiness requires that we should continue to mix with the world, & to keep pace with it as it goes; and that every person who retires from free communication with it is severely punished afterwards by the state of mind into which they get, and which can only be prevented by feeding our sociable principles.

## THOMAS JEFFERSON TO TUNIS WORTMAN, AUGUST 15, 1813

The **Specification** was Jefferson's view that the new newspaper will be successful and worthwhile. Later in the letter Jefferson will argue how to make a newspaper worthwhile.

> **Enunciation:** [**Given**] I return your subscription paper with my name willingly placed on it. [**Sought**] I have said <u>for one year</u>, and inclose the price, because I find myself happier in other branches of reading, than of newspapers.
>
> **Exposition:** I read 2. or 3. a week of the old ones still, but engage for no new ones; and have done it in your case, because I am confident it will be conducted in a good spirit,
>
> **Specification:** and I wish it therefore to be set agoing. I have no doubt it will afterwards stand firmly on it's own merits.

## ABRAHAM LINCOLN TO GEORGE ROBERTSON, AUGUST 15, 1855

Though the words are simple, the **Specification** contained a cryptic and jarring hypothesis regarding liberty. The **Specification** was shorter than the **sought**. Later in the letter Lincoln will argue the country's problematic view of liberty.

> **Enunciation:** [**Given**] My dear Sir: The volume you left for me has been received. I am really grateful for the honor of your kind remembrance, as well as for the book. The partial reading I have already given it, has afforded me much of both pleasure and instruction. It was new to me that the exact question which led to the Missouri compromise, had arisen before it arose in regard to Missouri; and that you had taken so prominent a part in it. Your short, but able and patriotic speech upon that occasion, has not been improved upon since, by those holding the same views; and, with all the lights you then had, the views you took appear to me as very reasonable.
>
> You are not a friend of slavery in the abstract. In that speech you spoke of "<u>the peaceful extinction of slavery</u>" and used other expressions indicating your belief that the thing was, at some time, to have an end[.] Since then we have had thirty six years of experience; [**Sought**] and this experience has demonstrated, I think, that there is no peaceful extinction of slavery in prospect for us.

**Exposition:** The signal failure of Henry Clay, and other good and great men, in 1849, to effect any thing in favor of gradual emancipation in Kentucky, together with a thousand other signs, extinguishes that hope utterly.

**Specification**: On the question of liberty, as a principle, we are not what we have been.

## ABRAHAM LINCOLN TO SAMUEL C. DAVIS AND COMPANY
## NOVEMBER 17, 1858

Looking for a way out, the **Specification** stated Lincoln will not continue to work for this client.

**Enunciation:** [**Given**] You perhaps need not to be reminded how I have been personally engaged the last three or four months. Your letter to Lincoln & Herndon, of Oct. 1st. complaining that the lands of those against whom we obtained judgments last winter for you, have not been sold on execution has just been handed to me to-day. [**Sought**] I will try to "explain how our" (your) "interests have been so much neglected" as you choose to express it.

**Exposition:** After these judgments were obtained we wrote you that under our law, the selling of land on execution is a delicate and dangerous, matter; that it could not be done safely, without a careful examination of titles; and also of the <u>value</u> of the property. Our letters to you will show this. To do this would require a canvass of half the State. We were puzzled, & you sent no definite instructions. At length we employed a young man to visit all the localities, and make as accurate a report on titles and values as he could. He did this, expending three or four weeks time, and as he said, over a hundred dollars of his own money in doing so. When this was done we wrote you, asking if we should sell and bid in for you in accordance with this information. This letter you never answered. My mind is made up.

**Specification:** I will have no more to do with this class of business.

## Abraham Lincoln to David Hunter, October 24, 1861

"Assuming this basis of fact," the **Specification** was the beginning of a precise strategy. Lincoln's suggestion to General Hunter was based on a hypothesis that permitted General Hunter to ignore it.

> **Enunciation:** [**Given**] Sir: The command of the Department of the West having devolved upon you, [**Sought**] I propose to offer you a few suggestions, knowing how hazzardous it is to bind down a distant commander in the field to specific lines and operations, as so much always depends on a knowledge of localities & passing events. It is intended therefore, to leave a considerable margin for the exercise of your judgment & discretion.

> **Exposition:** The main rebel army (Prices) west of the Mississippi, is believed to have passed Dade county, in full retreat upon North-Western Arkansas, leaving Missouri almost freed from the enemy, excepting in the South-East of the State.

> **Specification:** Assuming this basis of fact, it seems desireable, as you are not likely to overtake Price, and are in danger of making too long a line from your own base of supplies and reinforcements, that you should give up the pursuit, halt your main army, divide it into two corps of observation, one occupying Sedalia, and the other Rolla, the present termini of Railroads; then recruit the condition of both corps, by re-establishing, and improving, their discipline and instruction; perfecting their clothing and equipments, and providing less uncomfortable quarters.

## Euclid's Proposition 1

The **Specification** is more precisely stated than the **sought**:

> **Enunciation:** [**Given**] On a given finite straight line [**Sought**] to construct an equilateral triangle.

> **Exposition:** Let AB be the given finite straight line.

> A————————————B

> **Specification:** Thus it is required to construct an equilateral triangle on the straight line AB.

## QUESTIONS

ONE: What is the best (or most artful) **Specification** in this lesson? Why?

TWO: Is a hypothesis an opinion? Why?

THREE: Is a hypothesis a fact? Why?

FOUR: Is a hypothesis an argument? Why?

FIVE: What special quality does a hypothesis have? Explain.

SIX: The hypothesis in Euclid's Proposition 1 is that it is possible to construct an equilateral triangle on a finite straight line. How is that different from the other **Specifications** in this lesson? How does Proposition 1's **Specification** build from its **Exposition**?

SEVEN: How may the Investigation affect a **Construction**? How may the Investigation affect a **Proof**? What is the difference between how a **Construction** and **Proof** may be affected by an Investigation?

# CONSTRUCTION: ARRAY THE EVIDENCE

The **Construction** is the fourth of the six elements.

**Proclus definition:** "The **construction** adds what is lacking in the *given* for finding what is *sought*."[1]

### Address Delivered at the Dedication of the Cemetery at Gettysburg[2]
November 19, 1863

1. Four score and seven years ago our fathers brought forth on this continent, a new nation, conceived in Liberty, and dedicated to the proposition that all men are created equal.

Now we are engaged in a great civil war, testing whether that nation, or any nation so conceived and so dedicated, can long endure. 2. We are met on a great battle-field of that war. 3. We have come to dedicate a portion of that field, as a final resting place for those who here gave their lives that that nation might live. It is altogether fitting and proper that we should do this.

4. But, in a larger sense, we can not dedicate—we can not consecrate—we can not hallow—this ground. The brave men, living and dead, who struggled here, have consecrated it, far above our poor power to add or detract. The world will little note, nor long remember what we say here, but it can never forget what they did here.

It is for us the living, rather, to be dedicated here to the unfinished work which they who fought here have thus far so nobly advanced. It is rather for us to be here dedicated to the great task remaining before us—that from these honored dead we take increased devotion to that cause for which they gave the last full measure of devotion—that we here highly resolve that these dead shall not have died in vain—that this nation, under God, shall have a new birth of freedom—and that government of the people, by the people, for the people, shall not perish from the earth.

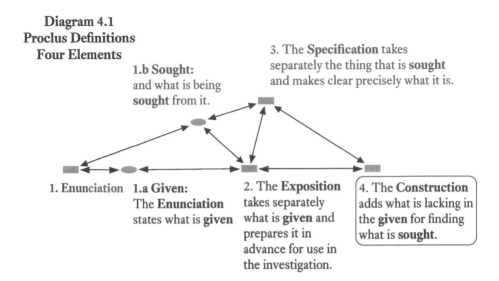

**Diagram 4.1**
**Proclus Definitions**
**Four Elements**

**1.b Sought:**
and what is being
**sought** from it.

3. The **Specification** takes
separately the thing that is **sought**
and makes clear precisely what it is.

1. Enunciation  **1.a Given:**
The **Enunciation**
states what is **given**

2. The **Exposition**
takes separately
what is **given** and
prepares it in
advance for use in
the investigation.

4. The **Construction**
adds what is lacking in
the **given** for finding
what is **sought**.

The **Construction** answers the question: *How do the facts lead to what is sought?*

**Function:** Without itself arguing, the **Construction** presented facts that set up argument to be made in the **Proof**. The **Construction** arrayed the evidence.[3] The Investigation framed the **Specification** and found facts to array in the **Construction**. A **Construction** normally should not venture beyond facts. The Gettysburg Address **Construction** may approach argument. It presented what the living and dead soldiers at Gettysburg accomplished. The **Proof** will argue additional action needed from the living to assure national survival.

**Tone:** A largely factual **Construction** should build directly into the **Proof**. The **Construction** may bend toward argument. It can do more than set up the **Proof**, but not much more. Ideally a reader or listener should be able to predict the **Proof** without the **Construction** arguing. Predicting the Declaration of Independence **Proof** (Lesson 16, pages 120-121) is easier than predicting the Gettysburg Address **Proof**.

> **Enunciation:** [**Given**] Four score and seven years ago our fathers brought forth on this continent, a new nation, conceived in Liberty, and dedicated to the proposition that all men are created equal. Now we are engaged in a great civil war, [**Sought**] testing whether that nation, or any nation so conceived and so dedicated, can long endure.
>
> **Exposition:** We are met on a great battle-field of that war.

**Specification:** We have come to dedicate a portion of that field, as a final resting place for those who here gave their lives that that nation might live. It is altogether fitting and proper that we should do this.

**CONSTRUCTION:** But, in a larger sense, we can not dedicate—we can not consecrate—we can not hallow—this ground. The brave men, living and dead, who struggled here, have consecrated it, far above our poor power to add or detract. The world will little note, nor long remember what we say here, but it can never forget what they did here.

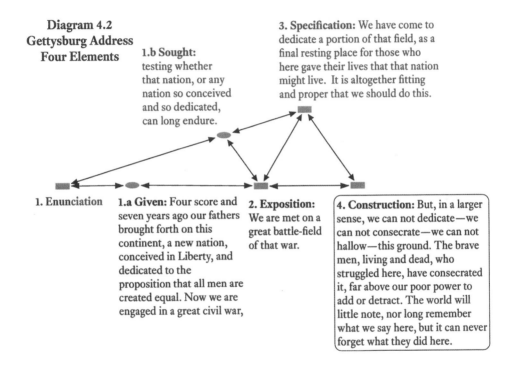

**Diagram 4.2
Gettysburg Address
Four Elements**

**1.b Sought:** testing whether that nation, or any nation so conceived and so dedicated, can long endure.

**3. Specification:** We have come to dedicate a portion of that field, as a final resting place for those who here gave their lives that that nation might live. It is altogether fitting and proper that we should do this.

**1. Enunciation**

**1.a Given:** Four score and seven years ago our fathers brought forth on this continent, a new nation, conceived in Liberty, and dedicated to the proposition that all men are created equal. Now we are engaged in a great civil war,

**2. Exposition:** We are met on a great battle-field of that war.

**4. Construction:** But, in a larger sense, we can not dedicate—we can not consecrate—we can not hallow—this ground. The brave men, living and dead, who struggled here, have consecrated it, far above our poor power to add or detract. The world will little note, nor long remember what we say here, but it can never forget what they did here.

A **Construction** can be simple or complex. It can be plain or innovative. It can be short or long. It should be largely fact. Even if complex, it must be clear (see **Construction** in Lincoln's Cooper Institute address first proposition, Lesson 16, pages 126-128). It should not directly argue. It should build into the **Proof**.

The Declaration of Independence **Construction** (Lesson 16, pages 118-120) arrayed more than two dozen facts. A **Construction** normally should not say more than is obviously true and necessary. Obvious truth can seem like understatement.

## Thomas Jefferson to John Stockdale, February 1, 1787

The **Construction** stated Jefferson's implied conditions for publication: no patent, and no edits.

> **Enunciation:** [**Given**] You have two or three times proposed to me the printing my Notes on Virginia. I never did intend to have them made public, because they are little interesting to the rest of the world. [**Sought**] But as a translation of them is coming out, I have concluded to let the original appear also.

> **Exposition:** I have therefore corrected a copy, and made some additions. I have moreover had a map engraved, which is worth more than the book.

> **Specification:** If you chuse to print the work I will send you the corrected copy, and when it shall be nearly printed I will send the plate of the map.

> **Construction:** I would not chuse that it should be put under a patent, nor that there should be a tittle altered, added, nor omitted.

## Thomas Jefferson to Henry Dearborn February 18, 1801

The **Construction** added the fact of Jefferson's delayed election February 17, 1801, on the thirty-sixth House of Representatives ballot. This letter was written the next day.

> **Enunciation:** [**Given**] The House of Representatives having yesterday concluded their choice of a person for the chair of the US. and called me to that office, [**Sought**] it now becomes necessary to provide an administration composed of persons whose qualifications and standing have possessed them of the public confidence, and whose wisdom may ensure to our fellow citizens the advantages they sanguinely expect.

> **Exposition:** on a review of the characters in the different states proper for the different departments, I have had no hesitation in considering you as the person to whom it would be most advantageous to the public to confide the Department of war.

> **Specification:** may I therefore hope, Sir, that you will give your country the aid of your talents as Secretary of war?

**Construction:** the delay which has attended the election has very much abridged our time and rendered the call more sudden & pressing than I could have wished.

## THOMAS JEFFERSON TO MARY JEFFERSON EPPES
## MARCH 3, 1802

The **Specification** stated, "I am convinced our own happiness requires that we should continue to mix with the world, & to keep pace with it as it goes…" The **Construction** presented a single fact: "I can speak from experience on this subject." In conclusory fashion, the **Construction** suggested Thomas Jefferson experienced the isolation he feared his daughter would suffer. The **Proof's** argument will be based on Jefferson's experience.

**Enunciation: [Given]** I observed to you some time ago that during the session of Congress I should be able to write to you but seldom; and so it has turned out. your's of Jan. 24. I recieved in due time, after which mr Eppes's letters of Feb. 1. & 2. confirmed to me the news, always welcome, of your's & Francis's health. since this I have no news of you. I see with great concern that I am not to have the pleasure of meeting you in Albemarle in the spring. **[Sought]** I had entertained the hope mr Eppes & yourself would have past the summer there. and being there, that the two families could have come together on a visit here. I observe your reluctance at the idea of that visit, but for your own happiness must advise you to get the better of it.

**Exposition:** I think I discover in you a willingness to withdraw from society more than is prudent.

**Specification:** I am convinced our own happiness requires that we should continue to mix with the world, & to keep pace with it as it goes; and that every person who retires from free communication with it is severely punished afterwards by the state of mind into which they get, and which can only be prevented by feeding our sociable principles.

**Construction:** I can speak from experience on this subject.

## THOMAS JEFFERSON TO TUNIS WORTMAN, AUGUST 15, 1813

In the **Construction**, Jefferson stated newspapers needed to redeem their character with credible, truthful information. He observed presently the truth itself becomes suspect when you read it in a newspaper.

> **Enunciation:** [**Given**] I return your subscription paper with my name willingly placed on it. [**Sought**] I have said <u>for one year</u>, and inclose the price, because I find myself happier in other branches of reading, than of newspapers.

> **Exposition:** I read 2. or 3. a week of the old ones still, but engage for no new ones; and have done it in your case, because I am confident it will be conducted in a good spirit,

> **Specification:** and I wish it therefore to be set agoing. I have no doubt it will afterwards stand firmly on it's own merits.

> **Construction:** a great object will be to redeem the character of our newspapers for falsehood, now so abandoned to it, that no one can believe, even probable things, at all the more for their being affirmed in a newspaper.

## ABRAHAM LINCOLN TO GEORGE ROBERTSON, AUGUST 15, 1855

In the **Construction**, Lincoln quoted a sentence fragment from the Declaration of Independence, "all men are created equal." It was a bridge from the **Specification** to the **Proof**.

> **Enunciation:** [**Given**] My dear Sir: The volume you left for me has been received. I am really grateful for the honor of your kind remembrance, as well as for the book. The partial reading I have already given it, has afforded me much of both pleasure and instruction. It was new to me that the exact question which led to the Missouri compromise, had arisen before it arose in regard to Missouri; and that you had taken so prominent a part in it. Your short, but able and patriotic speech upon that occasion, has not been improved upon since, by those holding the same views; and, with all the lights you then had, the views you took appear to me as very reasonable.

> You are not a friend of slavery in the abstract. In that speech you spoke of "<u>the peaceful extinction of slavery</u>" and used other expressions indicating your belief that the thing was, at some time, to have an end[.] Since then we have had thirty six years of experience; [**Sought**] and this experience

has demonstrated, I think, that there is no peaceful extinction of slavery in prospect for us.

**Exposition:** The signal failure of Henry Clay, and other good and great men, in 1849, to effect any thing in favor of gradual emancipation in Kentucky, together with a thousand other signs, extinguishes that hope utterly.

**Specification**: On the question of liberty, as a principle, we are not what we have been.

**Construction:** When we were the political slaves of King George, and wanted to be free, we called the maxim that "all men are created equal" a self evident truth;

## ABRAHAM LINCOLN TO SAMUEL C. DAVIS AND COMPANY
## NOVEMBER 17, 1858

The **Construction** contained a strong statement about what attorney Abraham Lincoln will and will not do.

**Enunciation:** [**Given**] You perhaps need not to be reminded how I have been personally engaged the last three or four months. Your letter to Lincoln & Herndon, of Oct. 1st. complaining that the lands of those against whom we obtained judgments last winter for you, have not been sold on execution has just been handed to me to-day. [**Sought**] I will try to "explain how our" (your) "interests have been so much neglected" as you choose to express it.

**Exposition:** After these judgments were obtained we wrote you that under our law, the selling of land on execution is a delicate and dangerous, matter; that it could not be done safely, without a careful examination of titles; and also of the <u>value</u> of the property. Our letters to you will show this. To do this would require a canvass of half the State. We were puzzled, & you sent no definite instructions. At length we employed a young man to visit all the localities, and make as accurate a report on titles and values as he could. He did this, expending three or four weeks time, and as he said, over a hundred dollars of his own money in doing so. When this was done we wrote you, asking if we should sell and bid in for you in accordance with this information. This letter you never answered. My mind is made up.

**Specification:** I will have no more to do with this class of business.

**Construction:** I can do business in Court, but I can not, and will not follow executions all over the world. The young man who collected the information for us is an active young lawyer living at Carrollton, Greene County I think. We promised him a share of the compensation we should ultimately receive.

## ABRAHAM LINCOLN TO DAVID HUNTER, OCTOBER 24, 1861

The **Construction** presented the necessity railroads remain under Union control.

**Enunciation:** [**Given**] Sir: The command of the Department of the West having devolved upon you, [**Sought**] I propose to offer you a few suggestions, knowing how hazzardous it is to bind down a distant commander in the field to specific lines and operations, as so much always depends on a knowledge of localities & passing events. It is intended therefore, to leave a considerable margin for the exercise of your judgment & discretion.

**Exposition:** The main rebel army (Prices) west of the Mississippi, is believed to have passed Dade county, in full retreat upon North-Western Arkansas, leaving Missouri almost freed from the enemy, excepting in the South-East of the State.

**Specification:** Assuming this basis of fact, it seems desireable, as you are not likely to overtake Price, and are in danger of making too long a line from your own base of supplies and reinforcements, that you should give up the pursuit, halt your main army, divide it into two corps of observation, one occupying Sedalia, and the other Rolla, the present termini of Railroads; then recruit the condition of both corps, by re-establishing, and improving, their discipline and instruction; perfecting their clothing and equipments, and providing less uncomfortable quarters.

**Construction:** Of course both Railroads must be guarded, and kept open, judiciously employing just so much force as is necessary for this.

## EUCLID'S PROPOSITION 1

Proposition 1's **Construction** built to its **Proof**. Despite the diagram and labels, the **Construction** was mostly words. The **Construction** of Proposition 1 literally used words to construct an equilateral triangle. It arrayed the evidence, or marshaled the facts, without arguing.

> **Enunciation:** [**Given**] On a given finite straight line [**Sought**] to construct an equilateral triangle.

> **Exposition:** Let AB be the given finite straight line.

> **Specification:** Thus it is required to construct an equilateral triangle on the straight line AB.

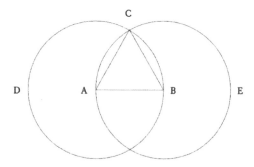

> **Construction:** With centre A and distance AB let the circle BCD be described; again, with centre B and distance BA let the circle ACE be described; and from the point C, in which the circles cut one another, to the points A, B let the straight lines CA, CB be joined.

## QUESTIONS

ONE: What is the best **Construction** in this lesson? Why?

TWO: What techniques to array the facts and marshal the evidence stand out in the **Constructions** in this lesson? How?

THREE: How are the facts in a **Construction** different from the facts in a **given** or an **Exposition**?

FOUR: While there is no prescribed length for a **Construction**, why might a **Construction** tend to be longer than the other five elements?

FIVE: How does one know when a **Construction** is the right size?

SIX: The Declaration of Independence (Lesson 16) **Construction** presented a lengthy array of grievances regarding unreasonable action and inaction by the King of Great Britain. How does the Declaration's lengthy **Construction**, which itself is not argument, leave little doubt what the short **Proof** that follows will argue?

SEVEN: Why does Proclus' definition of a **Construction** refer to the **sought** instead of referring to the **Specification**?

EIGHT: How do the words of a six-element proposition reveal its structure?

# PROOF: CONFIRM THE PROPOSED INFERENCE

The **Proof** is the fifth of the six elements. It is dependent on the four elements that precede it. **Proof** is the lynchpin of a six element proposition. The logical result from the **Proof** is the **Conclusion**. After the **Proof**'s scientific reasoning confirms the **Specification**'s proposed inference, the **Conclusion** recites what was demonstrated. At that point it becomes fact.

**Proclus definition:** "The proof draws the proposed inference by reasoning scientifically from the propositions that have been admitted."[1]

### Address Delivered at the Dedication of the Cemetery at Gettysburg[2]
### November 19, 1863

1. Four score and seven years ago our fathers brought forth on this continent, a new nation, conceived in Liberty, and dedicated to the proposition that all men are created equal.

Now we are engaged in a great civil war, testing whether that nation, or any nation so conceived and so dedicated, can long endure. 2. We are met on a great battle-field of that war. 3. We have come to dedicate a portion of that field, as a final resting place for those who here gave their lives that that nation might live. It is altogether fitting and proper that we should do this.

4. But, in a larger sense, we can not dedicate—we can not consecrate—we can not hallow—this ground. The brave men, living and dead, who struggled here, have consecrated it, far above our poor power to add or detract. The world will little note, nor long remember what we say here, but it can never forget what they did here. 5. It is for us the living, rather, to <u>be dedicated here to the unfinished work</u> which they who fought here have thus far so nobly advanced. It is rather for us to <u>be here dedicated to the great task remaining before us</u>—that from these honored dead we <u>take increased devotion to that cause</u> for which they gave the last full measure of

devotion—that we here <u>highly resolve that these dead shall not have died in vain</u> [underlining added]

—that this nation, under God, shall have a new birth of freedom—and that government of the people, by the people, for the people, shall not perish from the earth.

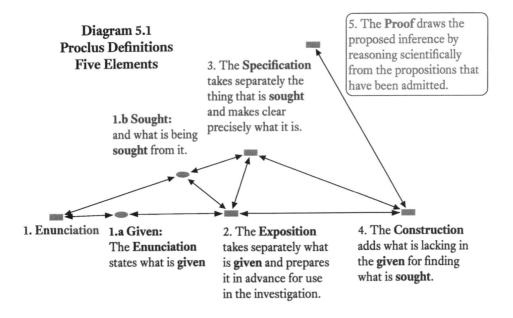

**Diagram 5.1**
**Proclus Definitions**
**Five Elements**

3. The **Specification** takes separately the thing that is **sought** and makes clear precisely what it is.

5. The **Proof** draws the proposed inference by reasoning scientifically from the propositions that have been admitted.

**1.b Sought:** and what is being **sought** from it.

1. Enunciation
**1.a Given:** The **Enunciation** states what is **given**

2. The **Exposition** takes separately what is **given** and prepares it in advance for use in the investigation.

4. The **Construction** adds what is lacking in the **given** for finding what is **sought**.

The **Proof** answers the question: *How does the admitted truth confirm the proposed inference?* **Specification**, proposed inference, and hypothesis, are synonyms.

**Function:** **Proof** (argument) reasons scientifically. It recites "what follows as a matter of reasoning."[3] Because a **Proof** is set up from admitted facts, it should be credible and seem self-evident. Lincoln's Gettysburg Address **Proof** argued what the living need to do for the nation to survive.

**Tone:** Straightforward, reasoned argument, based on what was set up. Flamboyance should not be necessary. One may be properly forceful, but must reason truthfully. Readers or listeners should react "of course," or at least make room for the possibility that the argument is correct.

> **Enunciation:** [**Given**] Four score and seven years ago our fathers brought forth on this continent, a new nation, conceived in Liberty, and dedicated to the proposition that all men are created equal. Now we are engaged in a great civil war, [**Sought**] testing whether that nation, or any nation so conceived and so dedicated, can long endure.

**Exposition:** We are met on a great battle-field of that war.

**Specification:** We have come to dedicate a portion of that field, as a final resting place for those who here gave their lives that that nation might live. It is altogether fitting and proper that we should do this.

**Construction:** But, in a larger sense, we can not dedicate—we can not consecrate—we can not hallow—this ground. The brave men, living and dead, who struggled here, have consecrated it, far above our poor power to add or detract. The world will little note, nor long remember what we say here, but it can never forget what they did here.

**PROOF:** It is for us the living, rather, to be dedicated here to the unfinished work which they who fought here have thus far so nobly advanced. It is rather for us to be here dedicated to the great task remaining before us—that from these honored dead we take increased devotion to that cause for which they gave the last full measure of devotion—that we here highly resolve that these dead shall not have died in vain

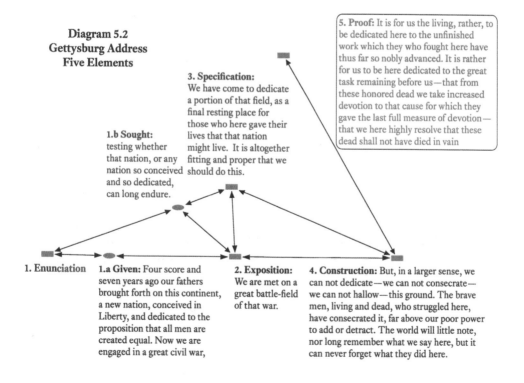

Diagram 5.2
Gettysburg Address
Five Elements

5. **Proof:** It is for us the living, rather, to be dedicated here to the unfinished work which they who fought here have thus far so nobly advanced. It is rather for us to be here dedicated to the great task remaining before us—that from these honored dead we take increased devotion to that cause for which they gave the last full measure of devotion—that we here highly resolve that these dead shall not have died in vain

3. **Specification:** We have come to dedicate a portion of that field, as a final resting place for those who here gave their lives that that nation might live. It is altogether fitting and proper that we should do this.

1.b **Sought:** testing whether that nation, or any nation so conceived and so dedicated, can long endure.

1. Enunciation

1.a **Given:** Four score and seven years ago our fathers brought forth on this continent, a new nation, conceived in Liberty, and dedicated to the proposition that all men are created equal. Now we are engaged in a great civil war,

2. **Exposition:** We are met on a great battle-field of that war.

4. **Construction:** But, in a larger sense, we can not dedicate—we can not consecrate—we can not hallow—this ground. The brave men, living and dead, who struggled here, have consecrated it, far above our poor power to add or detract. The world will little note, nor long remember what we say here, but it can never forget what they did here.

The **Proof** should matchup with the **sought** and **Specification**. If the **Proof** is not consistent with the **sought** and the **Specification**, something is wrong.

Thomas Jefferson wrote the Virginia Statute for Religious Freedom (Lesson 16) in the form of a six-element proposition. The statute itself demonstrated its need for enactment.

Virginia Statute's **Sought**: "<u>that</u> Almighty God hath created the mind free, <u>and manifested his supreme will that free it shall remain by making it altogether insusceptible of restraint</u>."

Virginia Statute's **Specification**: "and [attempts by coercion] are a departure from the plan of the holy author of our religion, who being lord both of body and mind, yet chose not to propagate it [religion] by coercions on either, as was in his Almighty power to do, <u>but to extend it by its influence on reason alone</u>."

Virginia Statute's **Proof**: Compelling "a man to furnish contributions of money for the propagation of opinions which he disbelieves <u>and abhors</u>, is sinful and tyrannical."

The rest of the Virginia Statute's extensive **Proof** argued for intellectual freedom. "…the opinions of men are not the object of civil government, nor under its jurisdiction."

## THOMAS JEFFERSON TO JOHN STOCKDALE, FEBRUARY 1, 1787

In the **Proof**, Thomas Jefferson argued his requirements for the map of Virginia. He asked whether Stockdale accepted the conditions for publication.

> **Enunciation:** [**Given**] You have two or three times proposed to me the printing my Notes on Virginia. I never did intend to have them made public, because they are little interesting to the rest of the world. [**Sought**] But as a translation of them is coming out, I have concluded to let the original appear also.
>
> **Exposition:** I have therefore corrected a copy, and made some additions. I have moreover had a map engraved, which is worth more than the book.
>
> **Specification:** If you chuse to print the work I will send you the corrected copy, and when it shall be nearly printed I will send the plate of the map.
>
> **Construction:** I would not chuse that it should be put under a patent, nor that there should be a tittle altered, added, nor omitted.
>
> **Proof:** It would be necessary to have a small half sheet map engraved of the country of Virginia as when first discovered. This map is only to be found

in Smith's history of Virginia, a thin folio, now very rare. I was not able to find that work here, but surely it can be found in London. An exact copy of the map is all that would be wanting. I leave this place about the 11th. or 12th. Be so good as to let me know whether you chuse to print this work under the conditions before named.

## THOMAS JEFFERSON TO HENRY DEARBORN
### FEBRUARY 18, 1801

The **Proof** argued the urgency of assembling a Cabinet. It expressed the desire that Dearborn act without delay.

**Enunciation:** [**Given**] The House of Representatives having yesterday concluded their choice of a person for the chair of the US. and called me to that office, [**Sought**] it now becomes necessary to provide an administration composed of persons whose qualifications and standing have possessed them of the public confidence, and whose wisdom may ensure to our fellow citizens the advantages they sanguinely expect.

**Exposition:** on a review of the characters in the different states proper for the different departments, I have had no hesitation in considering you as the person to whom it would be most advantageous to the public to confide the Department of war.

**Specification:** may I therefore hope, Sir, that you will give your country the aid of your talents as Secretary of war?

**Construction:** the delay which has attended the election has very much abridged our time and rendered the call more sudden & pressing than I could have wished.

**Proof:** I am in hopes our administration may be assembled during the first week of March, except yourself, and that you can be with us a few days after. indeed it is probable we shall be but a few days together (perhaps to the middle of the month) to make some general & pressing arrangements & then go home for a short time to make our final removal hither. I mention these circumstances that you may see the urgency of setting out for this place with the shortest delay possible, which may be the shorter as you can return again to your family, as we shall, to make your final arrangements for removal.

## Thomas Jefferson to Mary Jefferson Eppes
## March 3, 1802

In the **Proof**, Jefferson argued the ill effect he experienced from isolation.

**Enunciation:** [**Given**] I observed to you some time ago that during the session of Congress I should be able to write to you but seldom; and so it has turned out. your's of Jan. 24. I recieved in due time, after which mr Eppes's letters of Feb. 1. & 2. confirmed to me the news, always welcome, of your's & Francis's health. since this I have no news of you. I see with great concern that I am not to have the pleasure of meeting you in Albemarle in the spring. [**Sought**] I had entertained the hope mr Eppes & yourself would have past the summer there. and being there, that the two families could have come together on a visit here. I observe your reluctance at the idea of that visit, but for your own happiness must advise you to get the better of it.

**Exposition:** I think I discover in you a willingness to withdraw from society more than is prudent.

**Specification:** I am convinced our own happiness requires that we should continue to mix with the world, & to keep pace with it as it goes; and that every person who retires from free communication with it is severely punished afterwards by the state of mind into which they get, and which can only be prevented by feeding our sociable principles.

**Construction:** I can speak from experience on this subject.

**Proof:** from 1793. to 1797. I remained closely at home, saw none but those who came there, and at length became very sensible of the ill effect it had upon my own mind, and of it's direct & irresistible tendency to render me unfit for society, & uneasy when necessarily engaged in it. I felt enough of the effect of withdrawing from the world then, to see that it led to an antisocial & misanthropic state of mind, which severely punishes him who gives into it:

## THOMAS JEFFERSON TO TUNIS WORTMAN, AUGUST 15, 1813

The **Proof** presented four categorizations of truth that Jefferson argued a newspaper could use to restore press credibility. The argument included a reference to the autocracy of Napoleon.

**Enunciation:** [**Given**] I return your subscription paper with my name willingly placed on it. [**Sought**] I have said <u>for one year</u>, and inclose the price, because I find myself happier in other branches of reading, than of newspapers.

**Exposition:** I read 2. or 3. a week of the old ones still, but engage for no new ones; and have done it in your case, because I am confident it will be conducted in a good spirit,

**Specification:** and I wish it therefore to be set agoing. I have no doubt it will afterwards stand firmly on it's own merits.

**Construction:** a great object will be to redeem the character of our newspapers for falsehood, now so abandoned to it, that no one can believe, even probable things, at all the more for their being affirmed in a newspaper.

**Proof:** it is much better to publish late truths than early falsehoods. were I the publisher of a paper, instead of the usual division into Foreign, Domestic Etc I think I should distribute every thing under the following heads—1. True. 2. Probable. 3. wanting confirmation. 4. lies, and be careful in subsequent papers to correct all errors in preceding ones. at present it is disreputable to state a fact on newspaper authority; and the newspapers of our country by their abandoned spirit of falsehood, have more effectually destroyed the utility of the press than all the shackles devised by Bonaparte.

## ABRAHAM LINCOLN TO GEORGE ROBERTSON, AUGUST 15, 1855

In a powerful **Proof** Abraham Lincoln argued why a peaceful end to slavery was unlikely. Lincoln's argument included a reference to Russian autocracy.

**Enunciation:** [**Given**] My dear Sir: The volume you left for me has been received. I am really grateful for the honor of your kind remembrance, as well as for the book. The partial reading I have already given it, has afforded me much of both pleasure and instruction. It was new to me that the exact question which led to the Missouri compromise, had arisen before it arose in regard to Missouri; and that you had taken so prominent a part in it. Your short, but able and patriotic speech upon that occasion, has not been improved upon since, by those holding the same views; and, with all the lights you then had, the views you took appear to me as very reasonable.

You are not a friend of slavery in the abstract. In that speech you spoke of "the peaceful extinction of slavery" and used other expressions indicating your belief that the thing was, at some time, to have an end[.] Since then we have had thirty six years of experience; [**Sought**] and this experience has demonstrated, I think, that there is no peaceful extinction of slavery in prospect for us.

**Exposition:** The signal failure of Henry Clay, and other good and great men, in 1849, to effect any thing in favor of gradual emancipation in Kentucky, together with a thousand other signs, extinguishes that hope utterly.

**Specification**: On the question of liberty, as a principle, we are not what we have been.

**Construction:** When we were the political slaves of King George, and wanted to be free, we called the maxim that "all men are created equal" a self evident truth;

**Proof**: but now when we have grown fat, and have lost all dread of being slaves ourselves, we have become so greedy to be masters that we call the same maxim "a self-evident lie" The fourth of July has not quite dwindled away; it is still a great day—for burning fire-crackers!!!

That spirit which desired the peaceful extinction of slavery, has itself become extinct, with the occasion, and the men of the Revolution. Under the impulse of that occasion, nearly half the states adopted systems of emancipation at once; and it is a significant fact, that not a single state has done the like since. So far as peaceful, voluntary emancipation is concerned, the condition of the negro slave in America, scarcely less terrible to the contemplation of a free mind, is now as fixed, and hopeless of change for the better, as that of the lost souls of the finally impenitent. The Autocrat of all the Russias will resign his crown, and proclaim his subjects free republicans sooner than will our American masters voluntarily give up their slaves.

## ABRAHAM LINCOLN TO SAMUEL C. DAVIS AND COMPANY
### NOVEMBER 17, 1858

In the **Proof**, Lincoln presented an arrangement to allow him to properly cease representing this client.

**Enunciation:** [**Given**] You perhaps need not to be reminded how I have been personally engaged the last three or four months. Your letter to Lincoln & Herndon, of Oct. 1st. complaining that the lands of those against whom we obtained judgments last winter for you, have not been sold on execution has just been handed to me to-day. [**Sought**] I will try to "explain how our" (your) "interests have been so much neglected" as you choose to express it.

**Exposition:** After these judgments were obtained we wrote you that under our law, the selling of land on execution is a delicate and dangerous, matter; that it could not be done safely, without a careful examination of titles; and also of the <u>value</u> of the property. Our letters to you will show this. To do this would require a canvass of half the State. We were puzzled, & you sent no definite instructions. At length we employed a young man to visit all the localities, and make as accurate a report on titles and values as he could. He did this, expending three or four weeks time, and as he said, over a hundred dollars of his own money in doing so. When this was done we wrote you, asking if we should sell and bid in for you in accordance with this information. This letter you never answered. My mind is made up.

**Specification:** I will have no more to do with this class of business.

**Construction:** I can do business in Court, but I can not, and will not follow executions all over the world. The young man who collected the information for us is an active young lawyer living at Carrollton, Greene County I think. We promised him a share of the compensation we should ultimately receive.

**Proof:** He must be somehow paid; and I believe you would do well to turn the whole business over to him. I believe we have had, of legal fees, which you are to recover back from the defendants, one hundred dollars.

## ABRAHAM LINCOLN TO DAVID HUNTER, OCTOBER 24, 1861

The **Proof** contained President Lincoln's argument for the strategy he recommended General Hunter follow.

> **Enunciation:** [**Given**] Sir: The command of the Department of the West having devolved upon you, [**Sought**] I propose to offer you a few <u>suggestions</u>, knowing how hazzardous it is to bind down a distant commander in the field to specific lines and operations, as so much always depends on a knowledge of localities & passing events. It is intended therefore, to leave a considerable margin for the exercise of your judgment & discretion.

> **Exposition:** The main rebel army (Prices) west of the Mississippi, is believed to have passed Dade county, in full retreat upon North-Western Arkansas, leaving Missouri almost freed from the enemy, excepting in the South-East of the State.

> **Specification:** Assuming this basis of fact, it seems desireable, as you are not likely to overtake Price, and are in danger of making too long a line from your own base of supplies and reinforcements, that you should give up the pursuit, halt your main army, divide it into two corps of observation, one occupying Sedalia, and the other Rolla, the present <u>termini</u> of Railroads; then recruit the condition of both corps, by re-establishing, and improving, their discipline and instruction; perfecting their clothing and equipments, and providing less uncomfortable quarters.

> **Construction:** Of course both Railroads must be guarded, and kept open, judiciously employing just so much force as is necessary for this.

> **Proof:** From these two points, Sedalia and Rolla, and especially in judicious co-operation with Lane on the Kansas border, it would be so easy to concentrate, and repel any army of the enemy returning on Missouri from the South-West, that it is not probable any such attempt to return will be made before, or during, the approaching cold weather. Before spring the people of Missouri will be in no favorable mood to renew, for next year, the troubles which have so much afflicted, and impoverished them during this.

> If you adopt this line of policy, and if, as I anticipate, you will see no enemy in great force approaching, you will have a surplus of force, which you can withdraw from these points and direct to others, as may be needed, the railroads furnishing ready means of re-inforcing these main points, if

occasion requires. Doubtless local uprisings, for a time, will continue to occur; but these can be met by detachments, and local forces of our own, and will, ere long, tire out of themselves.

# EUCLID'S PROPOSITION 1

Euclid's Proposition 1 **Proof** was set up by its first four elements:

**Enunciation:** [**Given**] On a given finite straight line [**Sought**] to construct an equilateral triangle.

**Exposition:** Let AB be the given finite straight line.

**Specification:** Thus it is required to construct an equilateral triangle on the straight line AB.

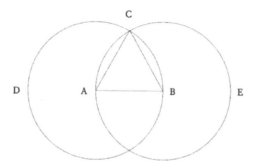

**Construction:** With centre A and distance AB let the circle BCD be described; again, with centre B and distance BA let the circle ACE be described; and from the point C, in which the circles cut one another, to the points A, B let the straight lines CA, CB be joined.

**Proof:** Now, since the point A is the centre of the circle CDB, AC is equal to AB. Again, since the point B is the centre of the circle CAE, BC is equal to BA. But CA was also proved equal to AB; therefore each of the straight lines CA, CB is equal to AB. And things which are equal to the same thing are also equal to one another; therefore CA is also equal to CB. Therefore the three straight lines CA, AB, BC are equal to one another.

## QUESTIONS

ONE: What is the best **Proof** in this lesson? Why?

TWO: How did the Jefferson and Lincoln demarcations in this lesson build from the first four elements to set up their **Proofs**?

THREE: How does the thoroughness of the **Construction** in the Declaration of Independence (Lesson 16) operate to make its **Proof** short?

FOUR: How does logic within a six-element proposition operate to turn a proposed inference into a fact?

# LESSON SIX: THE SIXTH ELEMENT

# CONCLUSION: WHAT WAS DEMONSTRATED?

The **Conclusion** is the sixth and last element.

**Proclus definition:** "The **conclusion** reverts to the **enunciation**, confirming what has been proved."[1]

### Address Delivered at the Dedication of the Cemetery at Gettysburg[2]
### November 19, 1863

1. Four score and seven years ago our fathers brought forth on this continent, a new nation, conceived in Liberty, and dedicated to the proposition that all men are created equal.

Now we are engaged in a great civil war, testing whether that nation, or any nation so conceived and so dedicated, can long endure. 2. We are met on a great battle-field of that war. 3. We have come to dedicate a portion of that field, as a final resting place for those who here gave their lives that that nation might live. It is altogether fitting and proper that we should do this.

4. But, in a larger sense, we can not dedicate—we can not consecrate—we can not hallow—this ground. The brave men, living and dead, who struggled here, have consecrated it, far above our poor power to add or detract. The world will little note, nor long remember what we say here, but it can never forget what they did here. 5. It is for us the living, rather, to be dedicated here to the unfinished work which they who fought here have thus far so nobly advanced. It is rather for us to be here dedicated to the great task remaining before us—that from these honored dead we take increased devotion to that cause for which they gave the last full measure of devotion—that we here highly resolve that these dead shall not have died in vain 6. —that this nation, under God, shall have a new birth of freedom—and that government of the people, by the people, for the people, shall not perish from the earth.

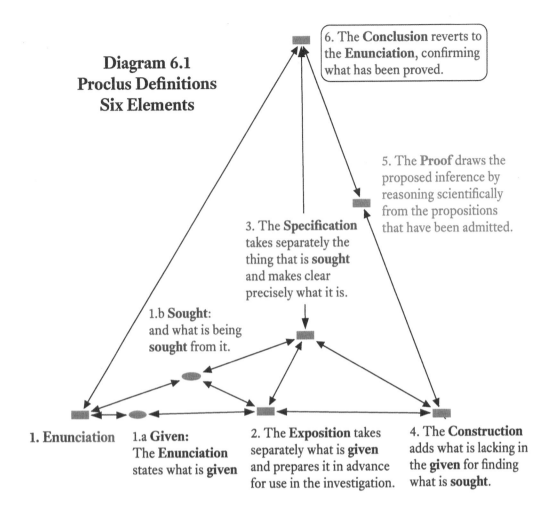

**Diagram 6.1
Proclus Definitions
Six Elements**

6. The **Conclusion** reverts to the **Enunciation**, confirming what has been proved.

5. The **Proof** draws the proposed inference by reasoning scientifically from the propositions that have been admitted.

3. The **Specification** takes separately the thing that is **sought** and makes clear precisely what it is.

1.b **Sought**: and what is being **sought** from it.

1. Enunciation

1.a **Given**: The **Enunciation** states what is **given**

2. The **Exposition** takes separately what is **given** and prepares it in advance for use in the investigation.

4. The **Construction** adds what is lacking in the **given** for finding what is **sought**.

The **Conclusion** answers the question: *What was demonstrated?* Gettysburg Address facts allowed credibility to grow. A self-evident **Proof** resulted in a solid **Conclusion**.

**Function:** The **Conclusion** was a firm, clear statement of what was demonstrated. Lincoln's *sought*, **Specification**, and **Conclusion** developmentally lined up. The **Proof** fit the *sought*, **Specification**, and **Conclusion**. Lincoln's **Conclusion** confirmed the likelihood that the living will finish the work necessary to preserve the Union. The nation, "conceived in Liberty, and dedicated to the proposition that all men are created equal," will likely endure. A cemetery dedication became a leadership opportunity.

**Tone:** Confident, clear, and accurate; ideally it should also reflect patience and humility.

**Enunciation:** [**Given**] Four score and seven years ago our fathers brought forth on this continent, a new nation, conceived in Liberty, and dedicated to the proposition that all men are created equal. Now we are engaged in a great civil war, [**Sought**] testing whether that nation, or any nation so conceived and so dedicated, can long endure.

**Exposition:** We are met on a great battle-field of that war.

**Specification:** We have come to dedicate a portion of that field, as a final resting place for those who here gave their lives that that nation might live. It is altogether fitting and proper that we should do this.

**Construction:** But, in a larger sense, we can not dedicate—we can not consecrate—we can not hallow—this ground. The brave men, living and dead, who struggled here, have consecrated it, far above our poor power to add or detract. The world will little note, nor long remember what we say here, but it can never forget what they did here.

**Proof:** It is for us the living, rather, to be dedicated here to the unfinished work which they who fought here have thus far so nobly advanced. It is rather for us to be here dedicated to the great task remaining before us— that from these honored dead we take increased devotion to that cause for which they gave the last full measure of devotion—that we here highly resolve that these dead shall not have died in vain

**CONCLUSION:** —that this nation, under God, shall have a new birth of freedom—and that government of the people, by the people, for the people, shall not perish from the earth.

Diagram 6.2 is a three-sided pyramid. The **given**, **Exposition**, and **Construction** are fact based. Everything coalesces as facts flow toward the **Proof** (argument). The result is a solid **Conclusion** with a firm structural base. In Diagram 6.2, our added underlining in the green elements highlights logical development. Relationships among the elements are dynamic, textured, and multidirectional.

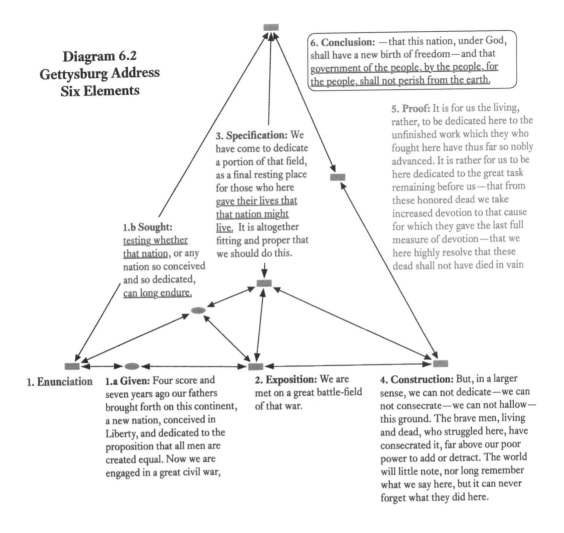

**Diagram 6.2
Gettysburg Address
Six Elements**

**6. Conclusion:** —that this nation, under God, shall have a new birth of freedom—and that <u>government of the people, by the people, for the people, shall not perish from the earth.</u>

**5. Proof:** It is for us the living, rather, to be dedicated here to the unfinished work which they who fought here have thus far so nobly advanced. It is rather for us to be here dedicated to the great task remaining before us—that from these honored dead we take increased devotion to that cause for which they gave the last full measure of devotion—that we here highly resolve that these dead shall not have died in vain

**3. Specification:** We have come to dedicate a portion of that field, as a final resting place for those who here <u>gave their lives that that nation might live.</u> It is altogether fitting and proper that we should do this.

**1.b Sought:** <u>testing whether that nation,</u> or any nation so conceived and so dedicated, <u>can long endure.</u>

**1. Enunciation**

**1.a Given:** Four score and seven years ago our fathers brought forth on this continent, a new nation, conceived in Liberty, and dedicated to the proposition that all men are created equal. Now we are engaged in a great civil war,

**2. Exposition:** We are met on a great battle-field of that war.

**4. Construction:** But, in a larger sense, we can not dedicate—we can not consecrate—we can not hallow—this ground. The brave men, living and dead, who struggled here, have consecrated it, far above our poor power to add or detract. The world will little note, nor long remember what we say here, but it can never forget what they did here.

A six-element proposition begins with general, indisputable facts, followed by a neutral, high-level statement of what is **sought**. The **Exposition** presents additional facts needed to perform the Investigation. The Investigation results in a **Specification** (the inference to be proved). It also results in facts arrayed in the **Construction** that lead into the Proof's argument. A scientifically reasoned Proof confirms the inference specified. A **Conclusion** recites what was demonstrated.

A skyscraper without structure topples no matter the quality of its steel and bricks. The same is generally true for a proposition. Gather and arrange facts for a firm foundation. Properly expressed facts in the right location are the steel and bricks that logic binds within a six-element proposition. Perfectly timed argument in the Proof leads to a credible **Conclusion** that structurally maximizes the likelihood of persuasion.

Relationships among the six elements can be tested:

The **sought**, **Specification**, and **Conclusion** should align. This involves focus and development. The **sought**, **Specification**, and **Conclusion** should progress in forcefulness from general, to specific, to firm:

1. A high-level, fairly neutral statement of what is **sought**.
2. A **Specification** clarifies what is **sought**; it is the proposed inference.
3. A **Conclusion** states the result of what was reasoned scientifically in the **Proof**.

President Lincoln's Second Inaugural Address (Lesson 16) had a high-level, impartial **sought**: "With high hope for the future, no prediction in regard to it is ventured." The **Specification** was more precise: "Each looked for an easier triumph, and a result less fundamental and astounding." The **Conclusion** included a firm view of the future:

> With malice toward none; with charity for all; with firmness in the right, as God gives us to see the right, let us strive on to finish the work we are in; to bind up the nation's wounds; to care for him who shall have borne the battle, and for his widow, and his orphan—to do all which may achieve and cherish a just, and a lasting peace, among ourselves, and with all nations.

In the Declaration of Independence (Lesson 16), **sought**, **Specification**, and **Conclusion** neatly line up.

> **Sought:** they should declare the causes which impel them to the separation.

> **Specification:** But when a long train of abuses and usurpations, pursuing invariably the same Object evinces a design to reduce them under absolute Despotism, it is their right, it is their duty, to throw off such Government, and to provide new Guards for their future security. Such has been the patient sufferance of these Colonies; and such is now the necessity which constrains them to alter their former Systems of Government.

> **Conclusion:** We, therefore, the Representatives of the united States of America, in General Congress, Assembled, appealing to the Supreme Judge of the world for the rectitude of our intentions, do, in the Name, and by Authority of the good People of these Colonies, solemnly publish and declare, That these United Colonies are, and of Right ought to be Free and Independent States; that they are Absolved from all Allegiance to the British Crown, and that all political connection between them and the State of Great Britain, is and ought to be totally dissolved; and that as Free and Independent States, they have full Power to levy War, conclude Peace, contract Alliances, establish Commerce, and to do all other Acts and Things which Independent States may of right do...

# Thomas Jefferson to John Stockdale, February 1, 1787

The **Conclusion** affirmed the manner of publication once the publisher accepted Jefferson's conditions.

Sir                                                                    Paris Feb. 1. 1787.

**Enunciation:** [**Given**] You have two or three times proposed to me the printing my Notes on Virginia. I never did intend to have them made public, because they are little interesting to the rest of the world. [**Sought**] But as a translation of them is coming out, I have concluded to let the original appear also.

**Exposition:** I have therefore corrected a copy, and made some additions. I have moreover had a map engraved, which is worth more than the book.

**Specification:** If you chuse to print the work I will send you the corrected copy, and when it shall be nearly printed I will send the plate of the map.

**Construction:** I would not chuse that it should be put under a patent, nor that there should be a tittle altered, added, nor omitted.

**Proof:** It would be necessary to have a small half sheet map engraved of the country of Virginia as when first discovered. This map is only to be found in Smith's history of Virginia, a thin folio, now very rare. I was not able to find that work here, but surely it can be found in London. An exact copy of the map is all that would be wanting. I leave this place about the 11th. or 12th. Be so good as to let me know whether you chuse to print this work under the conditions before named.

**Conclusion:** If I receive your answer in the affirmative before I set out, I will send you immediately the copy. It is an octavo of 391. pages. The American Atlas is come safe to hand. I am Sir your very humble servt.,

Th: Jefferson

P.S. It is not necessary to observe that as I have been at the expence of engraving the large map, I should expect to be paid for those you should have occasion for, a shilling a peice.

## THOMAS JEFFERSON TO HENRY DEARBORN
## FEBRUARY 18, 1801

The **Conclusion** expressed the hope Henry Dearborn would accept the appointment, which Dearborn did.[3]

Dear Sir                                                      Washington Feb. 18. 1801.

**Enunciation:** [**Given**] The House of Representatives having yesterday concluded their choice of a person for the chair of the US. and called me to that office, [**Sought**] it now becomes necessary to provide an administration composed of persons whose qualifications and standing have possessed them of the public confidence, and whose wisdom may ensure to our fellow citizens the advantages they sanguinely expect.

**Exposition:** on a review of the characters in the different states proper for the different departments, I have had no hesitation in considering you as the person to whom it would be most advantageous to the public to confide the Department of war.

**Specification:** may I therefore hope, Sir, that you will give your country the aid of your talents as Secretary of war?

**Construction:** the delay which has attended the election has very much abridged our time and rendered the call more sudden & pressing than I could have wished.

**Proof:** I am in hopes our administration may be assembled during the first week of March, except yourself, and that you can be with us a few days after. indeed it is probable we shall be but a few days together (perhaps to the middle of the month) to make some general & pressing arrangements & then go home for a short time to make our final removal hither. I mention these circumstances that you may see the urgency of setting out for this place with the shortest delay possible, which may be the shorter as you can return again to your family, as we shall, to make your final arrangements for removal.

**Conclusion:** I hope I shall not be disappointed in counting on your aid, and that you will favor me with an answer by return of post. accept assurances of sincere esteem & high respect from Dear Sir Your most obedt. & most humble servt

Th: Jefferson

## THOMAS JEFFERSON TO MARY JEFFERSON EPPES
### MARCH 3, 1802

The **Conclusion** affirmed that daughter Maria would be pleased with Washington society when she visited.

My Very Dear Maria                                    Washington Mar. 3. 1802.

**Enunciation:** [**Given**] I observed to you some time ago that during the session of Congress I should be able to write to you but seldom; and so it has turned out. your's of Jan. 24. I recieved in due time, after which mr Eppes's letters of Feb. 1. & 2. confirmed to me the news, always welcome, of your's & Francis's health. since this I have no news of you. I see with great concern that I am not to have the pleasure of meeting you in Albemarle in the spring. [**Sought**] I had entertained the hope mr Eppes & yourself would have past the summer there. and being there, that the two families could have come together on a visit here. I observe your reluctance at the idea of that visit, but for your own happiness must advise you to get the better of it.

**Exposition:** I think I discover in you a willingness to withdraw from society more than is prudent.

**Specification:** I am convinced our own happiness requires that we should continue to mix with the world, & to keep pace with it as it goes; and that every person who retires from free communication with it is severely punished afterwards by the state of mind into which they get, and which can only be prevented by feeding our sociable principles.

**Construction:** I can speak from experience on this subject.

**Proof:** from 1793. to 1797. I remained closely at home, saw none but those who came there, and at length became very sensible of the ill effect it had upon my own mind, and of it's direct & irresistible tendency to render me unfit for society, & uneasy when necessarily engaged in it. I felt enough of the effect of withdrawing from the world then, to see that it led to an antisocial & misanthropic state of mind, which severely punishes him who gives into it:

**Conclusion:** and it will be a lesson I shall never forget as to myself. I am certain you would be pleased with the state of society here, & that after the first moments you would feel happy in having made the experiment…

                                                    Th: Jefferson

## THOMAS JEFFERSON TO TUNIS WORTMAN, AUGUST 15, 1813

The **Conclusion** stated Jefferson's hope of success for Wortman's newspaper, and hope that it contribute to the restoration of credibility for the press.

Sir                                                             Monticello Aug. 15. 13.

**Enunciation:** [**Given**] I return your subscription paper with my name willingly placed on it. [**Sought**] I have said <u>for one year</u>, and inclose the price, because I find myself happier in other branches of reading, than of newspapers.

**Exposition:** I read 2. or 3. a week of the old ones still, but engage for no new ones; and have done it in your case, because I am confident it will be conducted in a good spirit,

**Specification:** and I wish it therefore to be set agoing. I have no doubt it will afterwards stand firmly on it's own merits.

**Construction:** a great object will be to redeem the character of our newspapers for falsehood, now so abandoned to it, that no one can believe, even probable things, at all the more for their being affirmed in a newspaper.

**Proof:** it is much better to publish late truths than early falsehoods. were I the publisher of a paper, instead of the usual division into Foreign, Domestic Etc I think I should distribute every thing under the following heads—1. True. 2. Probable. 3. wanting confirmation. 4. lies, and be careful in subsequent papers to correct all errors in preceding ones. at present it is disreputable to state a fact on newspaper authority; and the newspapers of our country by their abandoned spirit of falsehood, have more effectually destroyed the utility of the press than all the shackles devised by Bonaparte.

**Conclusion:** hoping that this evil may cure itself, by a wholesome application of the public countenance & patronage, and that you will have the merit of being instrumental to the restoration of value to this source of public information, I tender you my best wishes for success & the assurance of my esteem & respect

Th: Jefferson

## ABRAHAM LINCOLN TO GEORGE ROBERTSON, AUGUST 15, 1855

The August 15, 1855, letter to Kentucky Judge George Robertson is an early Lincoln writing that demarcates into six elements. **Sought** was to resolve a status quo of the unlikely peaceful extinction of slavery. The **Specification** asserted we have not been true to our original definition of liberty. This was backed up by the **Construction's** oblique reference to the Declaration of Independence. Lincoln's **Conclusion** asked, but did not answer, " 'Can we, as a nation, continue together permanently—forever—half slave, and half free?' The problem is too mighty for me." With greater determination, Lincoln repeated this question as an affirmative statement in the **Specification** of his 1858 House Divided speech.[4]

Surveyor Isaac Briggs visited Monticello in 1820.[5] Briggs described his conversation with Thomas Jefferson:

> Among other political points, that which has been called the Missouri question [slavery] stood prominent. He [Jefferson] said that nothing had happened since the revolution, which gave him so much anxiety and so many disquieting fears for the safety and happiness of his country. "I fear," said he, "that much mischief has been done already, but if they carry matters to extremities again at the approaching session of Congress, nothing short of Almighty power can save us. The Union will be broken. All the horrors of civil war, embittered by local jealousies and mutual recriminations, will ensue."[6]

In 1825, Jefferson stated regarding the abolition of slavery, "I leave it's accomplishment as the work of another generation."[7] Lincoln was from another generation.

Hon: Geo. Robertson                                        Springfield, Ills.
Lexington, Ky.                                               Aug. 15. 1855

**Enunciation: [Given]** My dear Sir: The volume you left for me has been received. I am really grateful for the honor of your kind remembrance, as well as for the book. The partial reading I have already given it, has afforded me much of both pleasure and instruction. It was new to me that the exact question which led to the Missouri compromise, had arisen before it arose in regard to Missouri; and that you had taken so prominent a part in it. Your short, but able and patriotic speech upon that occasion, has not been improved upon since, by those holding the same views; and, with all the lights you then had, the views you took appear to me as very reasonable.

You are not a friend of slavery in the abstract. In that speech you spoke of "the peaceful extinction of slavery" and used other expressions indicating your belief that the thing was, at some time, to have an end[.] Since then we have had thirty six years of experience; [**Sought**] and this experience has demonstrated, I think, that there is no peaceful extinction of slavery in prospect for us.

**Exposition:** The signal failure of Henry Clay, and other good and great men, in 1849, to effect any thing in favor of gradual emancipation in Kentucky, together with a thousand other signs, extinguishes that hope utterly.

**Specification**: On the question of liberty, as a principle, we are not what we have been.

**Construction:** When we were the political slaves of King George, and wanted to be free, we called the maxim that "all men are created equal" a self evident truth;

**Proof**: but now when we have grown fat, and have lost all dread of being slaves ourselves, we have become so greedy to be <u>masters</u> that we call the same maxim "a self-evident lie" The fourth of July has not quite dwindled away; it is still a great day—<u>for burning fire-crackers</u>!!!

That spirit which desired the peaceful extinction of slavery, has itself become extinct, with the <u>occasion</u>, and the <u>men</u> of the Revolution. Under the impulse of that occasion, nearly half the states adopted systems of emancipation at once; and it is a significant fact, that not a single state has done the like since. So far as peaceful, voluntary emancipation is concerned, the condition of the negro slave in America, scarcely less terrible to the contemplation of a free mind, is now as fixed, and hopeless of change for the better, as that of the lost souls of the finally impenitent. The Autocrat of all the Russias will resign his crown, and proclaim his subjects free republicans sooner than will our American masters voluntarily give up their slaves.

**Conclusion**: Our political problem now is "Can we, as a nation, continue together <u>permanently</u>—<u>forever</u>—half slave, and half free?" The problem is too mighty for me. May God, in his mercy, superintend the solution. Your much obliged friend, and humble servant

A. Lincoln—

## ABRAHAM LINCOLN TO SAMUEL C. DAVIS AND COMPANY
## NOVEMBER 17, 1858

The **Conclusion** firmly stated Lincoln would do no more business of the type this client expected.

Messrs S. C. Davis & Co                                     Springfield,
Gentlemen                                                   Novr. 17. 1858

**Enunciation:** [**Given**] You perhaps need not to be reminded how I have been personally engaged the last three or four months. Your letter to Lincoln & Herndon, of Oct. 1st. complaining that the lands of those against whom we obtained judgments last winter for you, have not been sold on execution has just been handed to me to-day. [**Sought**] I will try to "explain how our" (your) "interests have been so much neglected" as you choose to express it.

**Exposition:** After these judgments were obtained we wrote you that under our law, the selling of land on execution is a delicate and dangerous, matter; that it could not be done safely, without a careful examination of titles; and also of the value of the property. Our letters to you will show this. To do this would require a canvass of half the State. We were puzzled, & you sent no definite instructions. At length we employed a young man to visit all the localities, and make as accurate a report on titles and values as he could. He did this, expending three or four weeks time, and as he said, over a hundred dollars of his own money in doing so. When this was done we wrote you, asking if we should sell and bid in for you in accordance with this information. This letter you never answered. My mind is made up.

**Specification:** I will have no more to do with this class of business.

**Construction:** I can do business in Court, but I can not, and will not follow executions all over the world. The young man who collected the information for us is an active young lawyer living at Carrollton, Greene County I think. We promised him a share of the compensation we should ultimately receive.

**Proof:** He must be somehow paid; and I believe you would do well to turn the whole business over to him. I believe we have had, of legal fees, which you are to recover back from the defendants, one hundred dollars.

**Conclusion:** I would not go through the same labor and vexation again for five hundred; still, if you will clear us of Mr. William Fishback (such is his name) we will be most happy to surrender to him, or to any other person you may name. Yours &c   A. Lincoln

## ABRAHAM LINCOLN TO DAVID HUNTER, OCTOBER 24, 1861

This letter's **Conclusion** was the proposition's 58-word last sentence. It reinforced Lincoln's principles for battle decisions.

Washington, Oct. 24, 1861

**Enunciation:** [**Given**] Sir: The command of the Department of the West having devolved upon you, [**Sought**] I propose to offer you a few <u>suggestions</u>, knowing how hazzardous it is to bind down a distant commander in the field to specific lines and operations, as so much always depends on a knowledge of localities & passing events. It is intended therefore, to leave a considerable margin for the exercise of your judgment & discretion.

**Exposition:** The main rebel army (Prices) west of the Mississippi, is believed to have passed Dade county, in full retreat upon North-Western Arkansas, leaving Missouri almost freed from the enemy, excepting in the South-East of the State.

**Specification:** Assuming this basis of fact, it seems desireable, as you are not likely to overtake Price, and are in danger of making too long a line from your own base of supplies and reinforcements, that you should give up the pursuit, halt your main army, divide it into two corps of observation, one occupying Sedalia, and the other Rolla, the present <u>termini</u> of Railroads; then recruit the condition of both corps, by re-establishing, and improving, their discipline and instruction; perfecting their clothing and equipments, and providing less uncomfortable quarters.

**Construction:** Of course both Railroads must be guarded, and kept open, judiciously employing just so much force as is necessary for this.

**Proof:** From these two points, Sedalia and Rolla, and especially in judicious co-operation with Lane on the Kansas border, it would be so easy to concentrate, and repel any army of the enemy returning on Missouri from the South-West, that it is not probable any such attempt to return will be made before, or during, the approaching cold weather. Before spring the people of Missouri will be in no favorable mood to renew, for next year, the troubles which have so much afflicted, and impoverished them during this.

If you adopt this line of policy, and if, as I anticipate, you will see no enemy in great force approaching, you will have a surplus of force, which you can withdraw from these points and direct to others, as may be needed, the railroads furnishing ready means of re-inforcing these main points, if occasion requires. Doubtless local uprisings, for a time, will continue to occur; but these can be met by detachments, and local forces of our own, and will, ere long, tire out of themselves.

**Conclusion:** While, as stated at the beginning of this letter, a large discretion must be, and is, left with yourself, I feel sure that an indefinite pursuit of Price, or an attempt, by this long and circuitous route, to reach Memphis, will be exhaustive beyond endurance, and will end in the loss of the whole force engaged in it. Your Obt. Servt.

A. Lincoln

## EUCLID'S PROPOSITION 1

Euclid's Proposition 1 was demarcated into the six elements by Proclus over 1500 years ago. The **Conclusion** succinctly stated what was scientifically demonstrated:

**Enunciation:** [**Given**] On a given finite straight line [**Sought**] to construct an equilateral triangle.

**Exposition:** Let AB be the given finite straight line.

**Specification:** Thus it is required to construct an equilateral triangle on the straight line AB.

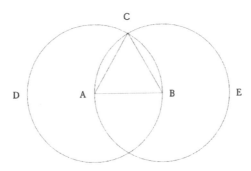

**Construction:** With centre A and distance AB let the circle BCD be described; again, with centre B and distance BA let the circle ACE be described; and from the point C, in which the circles cut one another, to the points A, B let the straight lines CA, CB be joined.

**Proof:** Now, since the point A is the centre of the circle CDB, AC is equal to AB. Again, since the point B is the centre of the circle CAE, BC is equal to BA. But CA was also proved equal to AB; therefore each of the straight lines CA, CB is equal to AB. And things which are equal to the same thing are also equal to one another; therefore CA is also equal to CB. Therefore the three straight lines CA, AB, BC are equal to one another.

**Conclusion:** Therefore the triangle ABC is equilateral; and it has been constructed on the given finite straight line AB. (Being) what it was required to do.

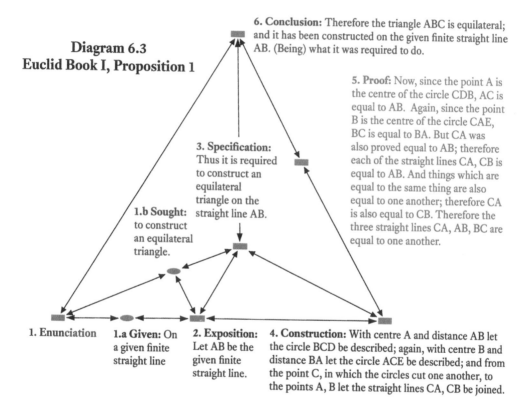

**Diagram 6.3**
**Euclid Book I, Proposition 1**

**6. Conclusion:** Therefore the triangle ABC is equilateral; and it has been constructed on the given finite straight line AB. (Being) what it was required to do.

**5. Proof:** Now, since the point A is the centre of the circle CDB, AC is equal to AB. Again, since the point B is the centre of the circle CAE, BC is equal to BA. But CA was also proved equal to AB; therefore each of the straight lines CA, CB is equal to AB. And things which are equal to the same thing are also equal to one another; therefore CA is also equal to CB. Therefore the three straight lines CA, AB, BC are equal to one another.

**3. Specification:** Thus it is required to construct an equilateral triangle on the straight line AB.

**1.b Sought:** to construct an equilateral triangle.

**1. Enunciation**

**1.a Given:** On a given finite straight line

**2. Exposition:** Let AB be the given finite straight line.

**4. Construction:** With centre A and distance AB let the circle BCD be described; again, with centre B and distance BA let the circle ACE be described; and from the point C, in which the circles cut one another, to the points A, B let the straight lines CA, CB be joined.

Diagram 6.3 is a pyramid that displays relationships among Proposition 1's six elements. Factually focused brown elements (the **given**, the **Exposition**, and the **Construction**) form one edge of the pyramid's base. The green **sought**, **Specification**, and **Conclusion** are a logical progression leading upward. The **Enunciation** (**given** and **sought**), **Exposition**, **Specification**, and **Construction** form the pyramid's base. The fifth element, the **Proof**, contains argument. A firm **Conclusion** results.

Euclid's Proposition 1 is a demonstration composed with words precisely placed inside six structural vessels. Six-element structure infuses words, sentences, and paragraphs with persuasive strength. Timing and credibility self-assert. The might of a demonstration is in its elements.

## QUESTIONS

ONE: What did the Gettysburg Address demonstrate?

TWO: What made the Gettysburg Address a great speech?

THREE: What is the connection between geometry and language?

FOUR: What is the best **Conclusion** from the examples in this lesson? Why?

FIVE: Is a **Conclusion** an opinion?

SIX: Is a **Conclusion** a fact?

SEVEN: What makes a **Conclusion** believable?

EIGHT: How do words work to establish a mathematical demonstration such as Proposition 1?

# THE METHOD IS THE MESSAGE

The story is in the words; the message is in the structure.[1] The six elements are a verbal form of the scientific method. The six elements of a proposition put together a demonstration by placing language in structured vessels. A six-element proposition begins with an **Enunciation** that contains a **given** and a **sought**. The **given** contains basic, indisputable facts. A neutral, high-level statement of what is **sought** is next. The **Exposition** contains additional facts needed to determine what to investigate. The **Specification** contains the hypothesis to be proved. Proclus referred to the **Specification** as the proposed inference.[2]

Evidentiary facts are arrayed in the **Construction**. It leads into the Proof's argument. The Proof reasons scientifically to confirm the **Specification**. A **Conclusion** recites what was demonstrated.

The **Enunciation**, Proof, and **Conclusion** are always required; the other three elements are not required.[3] Six elements provide full texture. For example, compare Thomas Jefferson's three element letter to John Pintard with his six element letter to Samuel M. Burnside (pages 109-110). Both letters demonstrate nearly the same thing. The six-element proposition is more robust.

This December 7, 1808, letter to Thomas Jefferson's grandson, Thomas Jefferson Randolph, regarding concise language appears undemarcated on page 7. It has six-element structure:

> Dear Jefferson                                      Washington Dec. 7. 08
> **Enunciation:** [**Given**] …The difficulty you experience in abridging the lectures is not unexpected. I remember when I began a regular course of study. [**Sought**] I determined to abridge in a common place book, every thing of value which I read.
>
> **Exposition:** at first I could shorten it very little: but after a while I was able to put a page of a book into 2. or 3. sentences, without omitting any portion of the substance.
>
> **Specification:** go on therefore with courage & you will find it grow easier & easier.

**Construction:** besides obligin you to understand the subject, & fixing it in your memory, it will learn you the most valuable art of condensing your thoughts & expressing them in the fewest words possible.

**Proof:** no stile of writing is so delightful as that which is all pith, which never omits a necessary word, nor uses an unnecessary one. the finest models of this existing are Sallust and Tacitus, which on that account are worthy of constant study.

**Conclusion:** and that you may have every just encouragement I will add that from what I observe of the natural stile of your letters I think you will readily attain this kind of perfection…

Th: Jefferson


This September 9, 1817, letter about plain English statutes to Joseph C. Cabell appears undemarcated on pages 7 and 8. It demarcates:

Dear Sir                                    Poplar Forest. Sep. 9. 17.

**Enunciation:** [**Given**] I promised you that I would put into the form of a bill my plan of establishing the elementary schools, without taking a cent from the literary fund. I have had leisure at this place to do this, & now send you the result.

if 12. or 1500. schools are to be placed under one general administration, an attention so divided will amount to a dereliction of them to themselves. it is surely better then to place each school at once under the care of those most interested in it's conduct. in this way the literary fund is left untouched to compleat at once the whole system of education, by establishing a college in every district of about 80. miles square, for the 2d grade of education, to wit, languages antient and modern, and for the 3d grade a single university, in which the sciences shall be taught in their highest degree. [**Sought**] I should apologise perhaps for the style of this bill.

**Exposition:** I dislike the verbose & intricate style of the modern English statutes, and in our revised code I endeavored to restore it to the simple one of the antient statutes, in such original bills as I drew in that work.

**Specification:** I suppose the reformation has not been acceptable, as it has been little followed.

**Construction:** you however can easily correct this bill to the taste of my brother lawyers, by making every other word a 'said' or 'aforesaid,' and saying every thing over 2. or 3. times,

**Proof:** so as that nobody but we of the craft can untwist the diction, and find out what it means; and that too not so plainly but that we may conscientiously divide, one half on each side. mend it therefore in form and substance to the orthodox taste, & make it what it should be; or, if you think it radically wrong, try something else, & let us make a beginning in some way. no matter how wrong;

**Conclusion:** experience will amend it as we go along, and make it effectual in the end. I shall see you of course at our stated Visitation, and hope all the gentlemen will consider Monticello as the rendezvous of the preceding day or evening. I salute you with friendship and respect.

Th: Jefferson

This March 19, 1822, letter about spelling to Horatio G. Spafford appears undemarcated on pages 8 and 9. It demarcates:

Dear Sir                                          Monticello Mar. 19. 22.
**Enunciation:** [**Given**] I duly recieved your favor of Feb. 28. and take a friendly interest in the good and the evil which you, as all our human brethren, have to encounter in the path of life. [**Sought**] I hope your literary labors will prove advantageous to yourself and useful to the world.

**Exposition:** the occupation of the mind is surely that which brings most happiness.

**Specification:** but with respect to your Apprentice's Spelling book, you could not have appealed to a more incompetent judge than myself.

**Construction:** I have never in my life had occasion to attend to that elementary stage of education, nor to reflect at all on the different methods of conducting it to best advantage.

**Proof:** this is a solid reason for my not undertaking to give an opinion on it, added to another which I have been obliged to lay down as a law to myself, of not usurping the right of saying to the public what is worthy or not worthy of their attention. this is the office of Critics by profession in whose line I am the least practised of all men living.

**Conclusion:** with my regrets therefore that I can offer nothing but my best wishes for the success of all your literary and other labors, accept the assurance of my esteem & respect.

Th: Jefferson

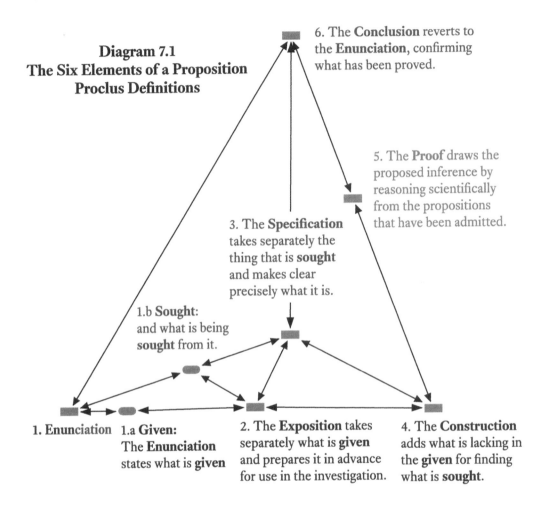

**Diagram 7.1**
**The Six Elements of a Proposition**
**Proclus Definitions**

6. The **Conclusion** reverts to the **Enunciation**, confirming what has been proved.

5. The **Proof** draws the proposed inference by reasoning scientifically from the propositions that have been admitted.

3. The **Specification** takes separately the thing that is **sought** and makes clear precisely what it is.

1.b **Sought**: and what is being **sought** from it.

1. Enunciation    1.a **Given**: The **Enunciation** states what is **given**

2. The **Exposition** takes separately what is **given** and prepares it in advance for use in the investigation.

4. The **Construction** adds what is lacking in the **given** for finding what is **sought**.

Solid facts within six-element structure build credibility. Perfectly timed, pinpoint **Proof** results.

All element definitions except the Proof directly refer to the **given**, the **sought**, or to both the **given** and **sought**, or to the **Enunciation** (which is composed of the **given** and **sought**). The **Enunciation** anchors synergies among the elements:

1. The **Enunciation** contains a **given** and a **sought**.
2. The **Exposition** refers to the **given**.
3. The **Specification** refers to the **sought**.
4. The **Construction** refers to the **given** and **sought**.
5. The Proof indirectly refers back to the **Enunciation**; the proposed inference is the **Specification** (or the **sought** if there is no **Specification**).
6. The **Conclusion** reverts to the **Enunciation**.

Testing structural relationships among the elements is helpful when drafting a proposition:

*Are the facts in the given basic and indisputable?* Facts are more important than logic. Without facts, there is nothing upon which logic can bind. The **given** should recite basic, obvious, indisputable facts that will build. Facts are established truth. If the facts of an unfinished writing are weak, consider adjusting the **sought** and **Specification**. The best facts are sometimes admissions from "the other side." See the first proposition of Abraham Lincoln's Address at Cooper Institute (Lesson 16, pages 125-126 and 130).

*Credibility.* Foundational fact grows credibility. Credibility by itself proves nothing. A provable **Specification** (hypothesis) is essential. Credibility permits an otherwise skeptical audience to make room for the possibility the proposition is correct.

*Is the sought higher level (more general), and more neutral than the Specification?* The **sought** may be general, and should appear impartial.

*Are the facts in the Exposition helpful and generally indisputable?* The **Exposition** recites additional facts necessary to conduct the Investigation. **Exposition** facts should be unquestionable: "And the war came." (Lincoln's Second Inaugural, Lesson 16, page 131).

*Do the given, and to some degree the Specification, err on the side of understatement?* Obvious truth sometimes seems like understatement.

*Is the Construction largely fact-based?* The **Construction** arrays facts that lead to the Proof. It is the equivalent of marshaling evidence. Stephen A. Douglas personally attacked Illinois U.S. Senator Lyman Trumbull's truthfulness with respect to a Trumbull speech. In Charleston, Illinois, at the Fourth Lincoln-Douglas Debate, Lincoln responded, "He [Trumbull] has only arrayed the evidence and told you what follows as a matter of reasoning."[4] Lincoln stopped just short of using the terms **Construction** and **Proof**. "Arrayed the evidence" describes a **Construction**. "Follows as a matter of reasoning" describes a **Proof** that confirms the **Specification's** proposed inference.

*Does the Construction smoothly lead into the Proof?* Ideally, by the end of the **Construction** the audience or reader will anticipate the **Proof**. A **Construction** can be innovative, but need not be. It can be simple or complex. It can be short or long. It should be largely fact based. It must be clear and understandable.

*Do the sought, Specification, and Conclusion align?* This checks focus and development. The **sought**, **Specification**, and **Conclusion** should line up. Each should focus the proposition at a different level:

1. **Sought:** A high-level, fairly neutral statement of what is sought. The **sought** makes the audience or reader a partner in the search for truth.
2. **Specification:** A clear statement of the hypothesis to be proved.
3. **Conclusion:** A firm, clear statement of what was demonstrated.

The **sought**, **Specification**, and **Conclusion** usually progress in forcefulness from general, to specific, to firm. There is room for measured, artful expression within a **Conclusion's** defined purpose.

*Is the Proof consistent with the sought, Specification, and Conclusion?* If the **Proof** is not consistent with the **sought**, **Specification**, and **Conclusion**, something needs to be fixed or adjusted.

*Are the Construction, Proof, and Conclusion strong, yet free of overstatement?* The **Construction** should not be argumentative. The **Proof's** scientific reasoning should be on point. The **Conclusion** should clearly state what was demonstrated.

Logically persuasive demonstration is best learned by drafting speeches, letters, or other compositions according to the six elements of a proposition. The more you do, the more natural it becomes. The six elements can alter the way you look at the world, and simplify the way you deal with it. The elements are bright lights on the path of reasoned persuasion:

**ENUNCIATION** "The **enunciation** states what is **given** and what is being **sought** from it."[5] The **Enunciation** states why a proposition is being addressed. The **given** contains objective, undisputed, agreed facts regarding the proposition. The **sought** presents a high-level, general statement of the problem. It is more impartially stated than the **Specification**.

EXPOSITION "The **exposition** takes separately what is **given** and prepares it in advance for use in the investigation."[6] Facts in the **Exposition** should be generally indisputable, appear neutrally stated, and channel the search for the truth. Proclus did not directly define "investigation," but the six elements are designed to state a problem and reason scientifically to a **Conclusion**. The **Exposition** expands from the **Enunciation** to focus or set Investigation parameters. Necessary facts in the **Exposition** channel the Investigation. The Investigation shapes the **Specification** and leads to arrayed factual evidence in the **Construction**. The **Exposition** itself is not the Investigation. The Investigation is mechanically invisible. But its parameters and results are vital and real to the scientific method. The **Specification** and **Construction** typically are products of the Investigation.

SPECIFICATION "The **specification** takes separately the thing that is **sought** and makes clear precisely what it is."[7] The **Specification** is a focused statement of the hypothesis to be proved. Ideally the Investigation should be complete before the **Specification** is drafted. While the **Specification** should not be overstated, it need not be neutrally stated. No matter how stated, the proposed inference must be provable. A proposition should flow naturally. During composition, a **Specification** may be drafted first, with the other five elements worked on in any order. While composing, the **Specification** should be regarded as a hypothesis subject to change.

CONSTRUCTION "The **construction** adds what is lacking in the **given** for finding what is **sought**."[8] The **Construction** is a product of the Investigation. It arrays factual evidence in preparation for the **Proof**. The **Construction** marshals the evidence. It should lead to a **Proof** that eliminates doubt.

PROOF "The **proof** draws the proposed inference by reasoning scientifically from the propositions that have been admitted."[9] Proclus did not expressly define "reasoning scientifically." **Proof** is a demonstration's muscle within a developed structure of logical reasoning. It should confirm the **Specification's** proposed inference. Though argument is in the **Proof**, the elements combine to reason scientifically. The result should be iron logic anchored in fact. The entire six element demonstration constitutes scientific reasoning. **Proof** is the muscle of a demonstration. Muscle is strong only because of what it binds to.

CONCLUSION "The **conclusion** reverts to the **enunciation**, confirming what has been proved."[10] The **Conclusion** usually is concise. It is always a clear statement of what was demonstrated. Its wording may be close to the **Specification**. It can be terse, but has reasonable literary flexibility. The **sought**, **Specification**, and **Conclusion** should develop and line up. The **Proof** must be consistent with the **Conclusion**. A straightforward sequence of established facts and persuasive evidence along with disciplined, self-evident argument, lead to a firm **Conclusion**. A mind disciplined in the six elements is sharpened for critical thinking.

## QUESTIONS

ONE: What is the connection between structure and credibility?

TWO: What is the connection between structure and persuasion?

THREE: How does structure convey meaning?

FOUR: Why are facts important?

FIVE: How do facts anchor a demonstration or proposition?

SIX: Thomas Jefferson's letter to his grandson Thomas Jefferson Randolph is demarcated into the six elements at the beginning of this lesson. The letter appears undemarcated in the workbooks's introduction. How does the demarcation add to understanding the letter?

SEVEN: What is the role of argument in a proposition? What is argument?

EIGHT: How do the elements combine or mesh synergistically? How do the structural mechanics work?

# WHAT'S IN A NAME?

After a two-year Congressional term, Abraham Lincoln was determined to elevate his oratory.[1] He burned the midnight oil reading Euclid's first six books. Between 1849 and 1854, he studied plane geometry.[2] Lincoln's goal was "to learn how to demonstrate."[3] During the five years after his two-year Congressional term Lincoln learned the six elements of a Euclidean proposition.[4]

Popular in Lincoln's time, Euclid fell out of favor in the twentieth century.[5] Popular or not, for at least the last few centuries mathematicians did not recognize the significance of the six elements of a proposition. Those who knew of the elements did not even agree on terminology. Translated from Greek, the elements of a geometric proposition were referred to as "regular stages" by James Gow in 1884,[6] "formal divisions" by Sir Thomas Heath in 1921,[7] "fundamental steps" by Edward A. Maziarz and Thomas Greenwood in 1968,[8] "elements" by Glenn Morrow in 1970,[9] and "parts" by Ian Mueller in 1981.[10]

Glenn Morrow's translation of Proclus' commentary on Euclid seems optimal:

> Every problem and every theorem that is furnished with all its parts should contain the following elements: an enunciation, an exposition, a specification, a construction, a proof, and a conclusion.[11]

1. **Enunciation:** "The enunciation states what is given and what is being sought from it."[12]

   The name "**Enunciation**" is clean and descriptive. It contains factual and logical roots to set the foundation.

2. **Exposition:** "The exposition takes separately what is given and prepares it in advance for use in the investigation."[13]

   "**Exposition**" is a good name. Its only weakness is the subtlety of its mandated function, the Investigation. It is deeper than its label's simplicity. The Investigation itself does not appear in the **Exposition** of a proposition. Only additional facts necessary to perform or frame the Investigation appear in the **Exposition**. The **Exposition** definition, in combination with the other five element definitions, cumulatively convey the **Exposition's** depth. If the Proof is the lynchpin of a proposition, the **Exposition** is its fulcrum.

3. **Specification:** "The specification takes separately the thing that is sought and makes clear precisely what it is."[14]

Clean. The "**Specification**" is a hypothesis.

4. **Construction:** "The construction adds what is lacking in the given for finding what is sought."[15]

Descriptive. The name "**Construction**" is clean enough. It takes time to appreciate its limitations. Its limits infuse strength. Arraying facts by marshaling evidence without argument is a powerful functional separation. Excellent examples are Euclid's Proposition 1, demarcated by Proclus (Lesson 6, pages 70-71), and the first proposition of Lincoln's Address at Cooper Institute (Lesson 16, pages 125-130).

5. **Proof:** "The proof draws the proposed inference by reasoning scientifically from the propositions that have been admitted."[16]

The name "**Proof**" is accurate. Clear up to a point, it can confuse. In a sense all six elements combine to "prove" or demonstrate. **Proof** as an element is more narrow. **Proof** as an element is perfectly positioned argument. Reasoning scientifically is descriptive, but not separately defined by Proclus. Confirming the proposed inference is understandable once one realizes the proposed inference is the **Specification**. The **Construction** arrays facts. The **Proof** is reasoned argument.

6. **Conclusion:** "The conclusion reverts to the enunciation, confirming what has been proved."[17]

"**Conclusion**" is an apt label, though its simplicity risks an initial impression that the elements are hardly deeper than beginning, middle, and end. The six elements are a verbal form of the scientific method, something much more robust and textured.

The six elements of a geometric proposition are not algebraic. Algebraic proof contains a sequence of statements (equations), more like a list than a paragraph. Each sequential algebraic statement is logical. The overall logic from the first algebraic equation to the last equation may not feel obvious. In a sense an algebraic proof is like getting to a destination by GPS. A word-based proposition is like knowing the route.

Plane geometry's six-element verbal orientation conveys a more tightly focused, tangible sense of overall reasoning than an algebraic proof. Six-element geometric structure builds a tight essay of verbal logic grounded in fact. It presents a cohesive, structured story in a way a collection of algebraic equations cannot.

A 1961 tenth-grade plane geometry textbook struggled with the concept of logical reasoning:

> We have said that theorems are going to be proved by logical reasoning. We have not explained what logical reasoning is, and in fact, we don't know how to explain this in advance. As the course proceeds, you will get a better and better idea of what logical reasoning is, by seeing it used, and best of all by using it yourself. This is the way that all mathematicians have learned to tell what is a proof and what isn't.[18]

The last sentence of the quoted paragraph is not true. If reason itself can't be articulated, how can it be called reason? Euclid, Proclus, Jefferson, Lincoln, and others mentioned in this book are human examples that show the tenth-grade geometry textbook is wrong. Two Greek mathematicians (Euclid and Proclus), and at least three American Presidents (Jefferson, Lincoln, and Obama), knew logical reasoning is definable. The "certain feel" of a well structured six-element demonstration is more than just feel. The six definitional sentences Proclus preserved, collectively define what creates the feel and performs the function.

United States Supreme Court Justice Potter Stewart cleverly fashioned a defective definition of pornography: "…I know it when I see it…"[19] A sound bite, no matter how clever, is not a demonstration.

The elements say what they are. They are what they say. Definition enables repeatable utility. The six elements of a proposition are a scientific method that can be used with civility for factually based, logically reasoned discourse and discussion of human problems.

## QUESTIONS

ONE: Explain how the six elements are or are not a verbal form of the scientific method.

TWO: If the six elements are a verbal form of the scientific method, does this denigrate science?

THREE: If the six elements are a verbal form of the scientific method, what does that reveal about science?

FOUR: What is the difference between an axiom and a fact?

FIVE: What is the difference between an axiom and faith?

# LETTER TO ULYSSES S. GRANT

Euclid's Proposition 1 constructed an equilateral triangle on a finite straight line.[1] Proclus demarcated that proposition into the six elements over 1,500 years ago (Lesson 20, pages 174-175). Over 700 Jefferson writings from 1776 on demarcate into the six elements.[2] Many Lincoln writings after 1853 demarcate. Many Obama speeches from January, 2011 on demarcate.[3]

Demarcation is the act of splitting a proposition into its elements. Demarcation is useful to better understand writings structured according to the six elements. Demarcation sharpens six-element composition skills, and sharpens critical thinking. There are at least two approaches to demarcating a writing that you know or suspect is structured according to the six elements of a proposition:

## Demarcation by Elimination

1. Identify the **Enunciation**, the first element. It is usually easy to spot the foundational facts of the **given** within the **Enunciation's** first portion. The latter portion of the **Enunciation**, the **sought**, should stand out because it identifies the general issue to be considered. The **sought** extends to the **Enunciation's** bottom edge. Mark the lines of separation.

2. The **Conclusion** is at the end of the document. Find the firm, positive statement that appears consistent with the **sought**. Mark the **Conclusion's** beginning.

3. Once the **sought** and the **Conclusion** are established, it should be easier to identify the **Specification**. The **Specification** is the hypothesis that the **Conclusion** affirms. Identify the **Specification**.

4. The **Exposition** is between the **Enunciation** and the **Specification**. Once the **Specification** is identified, the **Exposition's** boundaries are in place.

5. The start of the **Construction** is already marked, as is the end of the **Proof**. Find the line between the **Construction** and the **Proof**. Look for

the point where arrayed facts end, and argument begins.[4] That point fixes the beginning of the **Proof**.

6. Check each demarcated element to confirm each fits its definition.

## Top Down Demarcation

Top down starts at the top of a document and works straight down. It can be done by drawing demarcation lines with a pencil on a printed version of a document.

It may be easier to do electronically:

1. Create a template with a list of the six elements.

2. Paste the entire document into the first element (the **Enunciation**).

3. Read the text down to what appears to be the end of the **Enunciation**. Insert a blank line. Label the **given** and **sought** within the **Enunciation**.

4. At the beginning of the **Exposition's** text, type or paste the name "**Exposition**."

5. For better visibility, each of the six elements may begin on a new line. Continue the process, working sequentially to label the **Specification**, **Construction**, **Proof**, and **Conclusion**.

6. Check each demarcated element to confirm each fits its definition.

There is no one demarcation technique. No matter what the technique, the **sought**, **Specification**, and **Conclusion** should develop and line up. The **Construction** should array the evidence. The **Proof** should resolve what is **sought** by reasoning scientifically to confirm the **Specification's** proposed inference. The **Proof** should be consistent with the **Conclusion**.

Understand element definitions:

**Enunciation:** "The **enunciation** states what is **given** and what is being **sought** from it."—Proclus. The **Enunciation** answers the question: *Why are we here?*

**Exposition:** "The **exposition** takes separately what is **given** and prepares it in advance for use in the investigation."—Proclus. The **Exposition** answers the question: *What additional facts are needed to know what to investigate?*

**Specification:** "The **specification** takes separately the thing that is **sought** and makes clear precisely what it is."—Proclus. The **Specification** answers the question: *What must be demonstrated to resolve what is sought?*

**Construction:** "The **construction** adds what is lacking in the **given** for finding what is **sought**."—Proclus. The **Construction** answers the question: *How do the facts lead to what is sought?*

**Proof:** "The **proof** draws the proposed inference by reasoning scientifically from the propositions that have been admitted."—Proclus. The **Proof** answers the question: *How does the admitted truth confirm the proposed inference?*

**Conclusion:** "The **conclusion** reverts to the **enunciation**, confirming what has been proved."—Proclus. The **Conclusion** answers the question: *What was demonstrated?*

## LETTER TO ULYSSES S. GRANT

Abraham Lincoln's January 19, 1865, letter to General Grant is an example of Lincoln tact and restraint. Read it to gain the letter's sense. You will be asked to split the letter into the six elements.

Executive Mansion,Washington,[5]

Lieut. General Grant:                                          Jan. 19, 1865.

Please read and answer this letter as though I was not President, but only a friend. My son [Robert], now in his twenty second year, having graduated at Harvard, wishes to see something of the war before it ends. I do not wish to put him in the ranks, nor yet to give him a commission, to which those who have already served long, are better entitled, and better qualified to hold. Could he, without embarrassment to you, or detriment to the service, go into your Military family with some nominal rank, I, and not the public, furnishing his necessary means? If no, say so without the least hesitation, because I am as anxious, and as deeply interested, that you shall not be encumbered as you can be yourself. Yours truly

A. Lincoln

Separate the letter to General Grant into the six elements of a proposition, including both a **given** and a **sought** in the **Enunciation**. If you are stuck, look at **Hints** on the next page. Eventually, look at the suggested demarcation that follows **Hints**.

## Hints for Demarcation of the Letter to General Grant

Loosely stated, the **Enunciation** answers, "Why are we here?" The reasons for "being here" were based on indisputable facts (the **given**) and on seeking to resolve a general issue (the **sought**).

Since the **given** is the beginning of the **Enunciation**, and the **Enunciation** is the first element, the first sentence is likely part of the **given**. The letter's first sentence described how President Lincoln wanted General Grant to view Lincoln's upcoming request. The second sentence is factual and seems part of the **given**.

The part of the sentence after "Harvard" recited what Lincoln's son wished. The sentence beginning "I do not wish" contains Lincoln's decision criteria. The **sought** could begin at either spot ("wishes to see" or "I do not wish").

The **Exposition** presents facts needed to channel the Investigation. The sentence beginning, "I do not wish to put him in the ranks" refines and expresses Lincoln's state of mind. That is necessary for the Investigation.

"Could he, without embarrassment to you, or detriment to the service, go into your Military family with some nominal rank," is Lincoln's precise proposal. It fits the definition of a **Specification**.

A **Construction** is not required. The three required elements are **Enunciation**, **Proof**, and **Conclusion**. If there is a **Construction**, it must be "I, and not the public, furnishing his necessary means?" That is largely a fact regarding what Lincoln wanted to do. It is reasonable to label that sentence a **Construction**. One could also reason there is no **Construction**, and consider the sentence the beginning of the Proof.

The Proof surrendered control to General Grant regarding the proposition's resolution: "If no, say so without the least hesitation…" The Commander in Chief surrendered control to his General. This Proof is a direct extension of the **given**.

Since a **Conclusion** is a required element, it must be, "because I am as anxious, and as deeply interested, that you shall not be encumbered as you can be yourself." It affirms Lincoln's surrender of control.

This artful letter persuasively uses the elements of a proposition.

## Suggested Demarcation of Letter to Ulysses S. Grant

Executive Mansion, Washington,

Lieut. General Grant:                                                    Jan. 19, 1865.

**Enunciation:** [**Given**] Please read and answer this letter as though I was not President, but only a friend. My son, now in his twenty second year, having graduated at Harvard, [**Sought**] wishes to see something of the war before it ends.

**Exposition:** I do not wish to put him in the ranks, nor yet to give him a commission, to which those who have already served long, are better entitled, and better qualified to hold.

**Specification:** Could he, without embarrassment to you, or detriment to the service, go into your Military family with some nominal rank,

**Construction:** I, and not the public, furnishing his necessary means?

**Proof:** If no, say so without the least hesitation,

**Conclusion:** because I am as anxious, and as deeply interested, that you shall not be encumbered as you can be yourself. Yours truly.

A. Lincoln

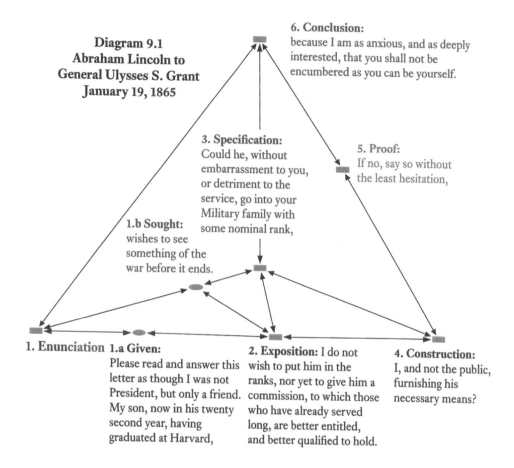

**Diagram 9.1**
**Abraham Lincoln to**
**General Ulysses S. Grant**
**January 19, 1865**

**6. Conclusion:**
because I am as anxious, and as deeply interested, that you shall not be encumbered as you can be yourself.

**3. Specification:**
Could he, without embarrassment to you, or detriment to the service, go into your Military family with some nominal rank,

**5. Proof:**
If no, say so without the least hesitation,

**1.b Sought:**
wishes to see something of the war before it ends.

**1. Enunciation**

**1.a Given:**
Please read and answer this letter as though I was not President, but only a friend. My son, now in his twenty second year, having graduated at Harvard,

**2. Exposition:** I do not wish to put him in the ranks, nor yet to give him a commission, to which those who have already served long, are better entitled, and better qualified to hold.

**4. Construction:**
I, and not the public, furnishing his necessary means?

## DEMONSTRATION

**Enunciation**: [**Given**] In order to learn how to compose according to the six elements of a proposition, it is useful to understand how to demarcate the writing of others who used the elements, such as Thomas Jefferson, Abraham Lincoln, and Barack Obama. [**Sought**] A six element proposition sets out to demonstrate. A proposition is a factually based presentation that is logically structured to lead, teach, or persuade.

**Exposition**: A thorough understanding of six-element-function should be internalized. Proclus demarcated Euclid's first proposition into the six elements over 1500 years ago. Euclid's first proposition demonstrated how to construct an equilateral triangle on a finite straight line. With practice you will be able to sense communication that demarcates. Most writings and speeches today do not. This lesson contains strategies for decomposition of writings that are known to demarcate, or are likely to demarcate.

**Specification**: The strategies presented make demarcation easier. The more you demarcate, and the more you deeply think about element definitions, the more persuasive skills develop. Argument can be the smallest part of persuasion. Yet argument or proof can be the hardest to perfect. Argument is a proposition's punch line. Weakness in any element is likely to make scientific reasoning more difficult.

**Construction**: It is axiomatic that the **Enunciation** is the first element, and the **Conclusion** the last. The **Specification** should be similar to the **Conclusion**. The **sought** generally is broader and more neutral than the **Specification**. The uncontroverted fact of the **Exposition** is after the **sought**, and before the **Specification**. The **Construction** is after the **Specification**. The **Construction** largely arrays facts that lead into the **Proof**.

**Proof**: The definitions of the six elements provide the ultimate standards for demarcation. Each element should function according to its defined purpose. Cross checks are useful in testing purpose.

**Conclusion**: Demonstration requires credibility. Location builds credibility. Location is timing. Argument is the punch line of persuasion. The **Conclusion** states what was demonstrated.

## QUESTIONS

ONE: How do the six elements of a proposition make Abraham Lincoln's letter to General Grant special?

TWO: What is the definition of critical thinking?

THREE: Why is critical thinking important to the six elements of a proposition?

FOUR: Would President Lincoln have been an effective leader without the six elements of a proposition?

FIVE: Without the six elements of a proposition, would Lincoln have become President?

# LINCOLN'S FAREWELL ADDRESS

Attorney Isaac Newton Arnold described the Lincoln-Douglas debates. Arnold contrasted Stephen A. Douglas, an Aristotelian do-whatever-works rhetorician, with Abraham Lincoln, a student of geometric, structured logic:

> Douglas carried away the most popular applause, but Lincoln made the deeper and more lasting impression. Douglas did not disdain an immediate, ad captandum [emotionally pandered] triumph, while Lincoln aimed at permanent conviction. Sometimes, when Lincoln's friends urged him to raise a storm of applause, which he could always do, by his happy illustrations and amusing stories, he refused, saying the occasion was too serious, the issue too grave. "I do not seek applause," said he, "nor to amuse the people, I want to convince them."
>
> It was often observed during this canvass, that, while Douglas was sometimes greeted with the loudest cheers, when Lincoln closed, the people seemed solemn and serious, and could be heard, all through the crowd, gravely and anxiously discussing the topics on which he had been speaking.[1]

Composition of a persuasive writing or speech within the six elements of a proposition focuses on facts carefully meshed with logic to properly form a hypothesis, and scientifically confirm it. The six elements are vessels of a living demonstration. The location of a sentence or paragraph is at least as important as its words. Location controls function, and enforces timing.

Words within six-element structure live as a result of their location. The six elements of a proposition naturally structure logical persuasion. Each element is a vessel that words must qualify to occupy. Each of the six vessels has a unique function for the words it contains. Radiating structural synergy, perfect timing leverages persuasion. The meaning of the location is as important as the meaning of the word. Because organization pre-exists, reorganization is reduced. Writer's block should nearly vanish. There should be steady progress. For instance, the most delicate part of a demonstration is argument. The six elements make argument composition (the **Proof**) easier.

Interrupt driven time-use is natural during six-element composition. The power of locational structure enables use of even tiny time segments to work on any element. Element location within a structured draft assists memory of purpose and memory of past state of mind. It is easier to resume writing after an interruption. Five or ten minute time segments become productive. Efficient time use is maximized.

A **Specification** is dependent on facts in other elements. The first four elements determine the limits on what can be demonstrated. In some situations a **Specification** must be modified to articulate a viable hypothesis. The six elements do not guarantee a Gettysburg Address. Neither do the elements guarantee persuasion, particularly when on the "wrong side" of an issue. Properly used, the six elements maximize the possibility to convince and to lead.

## LINCOLN'S SPRINGFIELD FAREWELL ADDRESS

Abraham Lincoln's 152 word February 11, 1861, farewell at Springfield's Great Western Station creatively used the six elements of a proposition to say goodbye. Lincoln then left for Washington to be sworn in as the 16th President of the United States. He did not return alive:

> My friends—No one, not in my situation, can appreciate my feeling of sadness at this parting. To this place, and the kindness of these people, I owe every thing. Here I have lived a quarter of a century, and have passed from a young to an old man. Here my children have been born, and one is buried. I now leave, not knowing when, or whether ever, I may return, with a task before me greater than that which rested upon Washington. Without the assistance of that Divine Being, who ever attended him, I cannot succeed. With that assistance I cannot fail. Trusting in Him, who can go with me, and remain with you and be every where for good, let us confidently hope that all will yet be well. To His care commending you, as I hope in your prayers you will commend me, I bid you an affectionate farewell.[2]

Demarcate the speech. **Hints** on the next page precede the suggested demarcation.

## Hints for Demarcation of Lincoln's Farewell Address

Within the **Enunciation**, the **given** begins with a fundamental fact about Lincoln's farewell. This succinct speech perhaps has a one word **sought** that broadly frames the proposition.

The **Exposition** adds facts needed to perform the Investigation.

The **Specification** focuses the significance of Lincoln's departure. It emphasizes the future's uncertainty.

The **Construction** adds facts for finding what is **sought**. It frames the task Lincoln confronts.

The **Proof** indicates what is necessary for success.

The **Conclusion** restates the theme of the proposition, and affirms what was proved: both "an affectionate farewell" and prayer. Prayer relates back to the uncertain future alluded to in the **Specification**, and is a direct extension of what was proved. The **Specification** and the **Conclusion** are parallel.

## Suggested Demarcation of Lincoln's Farewell Address

**Enunciation:** [**Given**] My friends—No one, not in my situation, can appreciate my feeling of sadness at this [**Sought**] parting.

**Exposition:** To this place, and the kindness of these people, I owe every thing. Here I have lived a quarter of a century, and have passed from a young to an old man. Here my children have been born, and one is buried.

**Specification:** I now leave, not knowing when, or whether ever, I may return,

**Construction:** with a task before me greater than that which rested upon Washington.

**Proof:** Without the assistance of that Divine Being, who ever attended him, I cannot succeed. With that assistance I cannot fail. Trusting in Him, who can go with me, and remain with you and be every where for good, let us confidently hope that all will yet be well.

**Conclusion:** To His care commending you, as I hope in your prayers you will commend me, I bid you an affectionate farewell.

Lincoln creatively turned a goodbye into a leadership opportunity. Every creative choice is a chance to be misunderstood. Creativity risks disconnects. Six-element structure provides purpose, place, and time for measured creativity. The elements modulate creativity to produce measured beauty. Risk of disconnect is reduced.

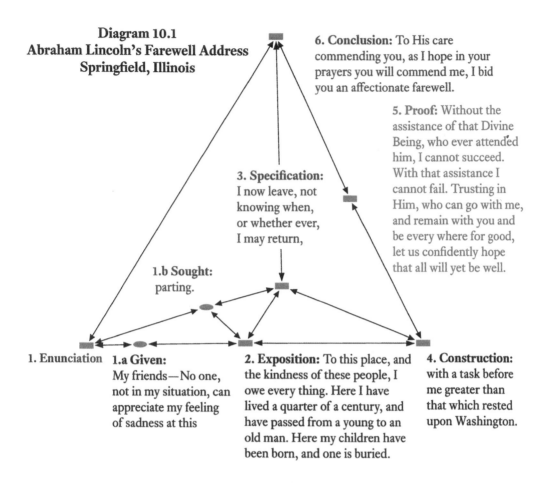

Diagram 10.1
Abraham Lincoln's Farewell Address
Springfield, Illinois

6. Conclusion: To His care commending you, as I hope in your prayers you will commend me, I bid you an affectionate farewell.

5. Proof: Without the assistance of that Divine Being, who ever attended him, I cannot succeed. With that assistance I cannot fail. Trusting in Him, who can go with me, and remain with you and be every where for good, let us confidently hope that all will yet be well.

3. Specification: I now leave, not knowing when, or whether ever, I may return,

1.b Sought: parting.

1. Enunciation

1.a Given: My friends—No one, not in my situation, can appreciate my feeling of sadness at this

2. Exposition: To this place, and the kindness of these people, I owe every thing. Here I have lived a quarter of a century, and have passed from a young to an old man. Here my children have been born, and one is buried.

4. Construction: with a task before me greater than that which rested upon Washington.

The Farewell Address **sought** was general, high-level: "parting." The **Specification** focused: "I now leave, not knowing when, or whether ever, I may return." The **Proof** presented mutual uncertainty which Lincoln and the people of Springfield must confront. The **Proof** was consistent with the **sought** and **Specification**. The **Conclusion** firmly stated what was demonstrated: An affectionate farewell, and the need for prayer to deal with mutual uncertainty.

## A Living Demonstration

**Enunciation**: [**Given**] The most important benefit of the six elements of a proposition is a scientific method of persuasive structure. Other benefits include time saved, and the ability to work effectively in interrupt mode. [**Sought**] The six elements are vessels of a living demonstration.

**Exposition**: Location nourishes.

**Specification**: Facts and logic live within a six element proposition.

**Construction**: A demonstration properly done is like a warm handshake.

**Proof**: The power of six-element locational structure is natural timing with proper modulation. Factual foundation and logical development are nearly automatic.

**Conclusion**: Argument rests on facts and logic. A credible **Proof** and a successful demonstration are more likely. Civility and persuasion are natural.

## Questions

ONE: What is the difference between argument and demonstration?

TWO: How does one spot weakness in an argument?

THREE: How does one spot weakness in a demonstration?

FOUR: How do the six elements of a proposition make Abraham Lincoln's Farewell Address special?

FIVE: Compared to other composition techniques, what effect do the six elements have on the number of necessary words?

SIX: What is logic?

SEVEN: What is the role of structure in a demonstration?

EIGHT: What makes a demonstration special?

NINE: How is a poem made special?

# THE INVESTIGATION

The Investigation develops facts. It is just as important to understand facts that seem to weaken a proposition, as those that seem to support it. Abraham Lincoln's third law partner, William Herndon, subscribed to abolitionist newspapers. Lincoln wanted Southern newspapers.[1]

> Lincoln and I took such papers as the Chicago *Tribune*, New York *Tribune, Anti-Slavery Standard, Emancipator*, and *National Era*. On the other side of the question we took the Charleston *Mercury* and the Richmond *Enquirer*.[2]

Logic has no force without facts. If a six element proposition is the gun, facts are the ammunition. The **Exposition** presents facts additional to the **given** that are needed to know what to investigate.

Herndon commented on Lincoln's reasoning:

> He [Lincoln] reasoned from well-chosen principles with such clearness, force, and directness that the tallest intellects in the land bowed to him. He was the strongest man I ever saw, looking at him from the elevated standpoint of reason and logic. He came down from that height with irresistible and crashing force. His Cooper Institute and other printed speeches will prove this; but his speeches before the courts—especially the Supreme Court of Illinois—if they had been preserved, would demonstrate it still more plainly. Here he demanded time to think and prepare. The office of reason is to determine the truth. Truth is the power of reason, and Lincoln loved truth for its own sake. It was to him reason's food.[3]

Truth and fact are essential building blocks. The Investigation, mentioned only in the **Exposition's** definition, focuses facts and pushes words to their proper place. The builder of a six-element proposition can't control the facts, but can control the quality of factual research. Structured within the six elements, facts and critical thinking push to a scientifically reasoned **Conclusion**.

The Investigation directly influences the **Exposition**, **Specification**, and **Construction**. It at least indirectly influences the **Enunciation**, Proof, and **Conclusion**. The Investigation feeds scientific reasoning.

Herndon wrote regarding Lincoln's invitation to speak at Cooper Union:

> In the preceding October [1859] he [Lincoln] came rushing into the office one morning, with the letter from New York City, inviting him to deliver a lecture there, and asked my advice and that of other friends as to the subject and character of his address. We all recommended a speech on the political situation. Remembering his poor success as a lecturer himself, he adopted our suggestions. He accepted the invitation of the New York committee, at the same time notifying them that his speech would deal entirely with political questions, and fixing a day late in February as the most convenient time. Meanwhile he spent the intervening time in careful preparation. He searched through the dusty volumes of congressional proceedings in the State library, and dug deeply into political history.[4]

According to Yale law professor John P. Frank the February 27, 1860, New York City Address at Cooper Institute, "…was perhaps the most thoroughly prepared speech Lincoln ever made…"[5] Lincoln spent over three months researching his 90 minute address.[6] The address persuaded eastern Republicans he was a viable candidate for the 1860 presidential nomination.[7]

Lincoln's Cooper Union address contained three six-element propositions. The first proposition argued Stephen A. Douglas was wrong. Lincoln constructed a creative demonstration that the federal government could constitutionally regulate slavery in the territories. See Lesson 16 for the first proposition of the Address at Cooper Institute. The second proposition argued the 1857 U.S. Supreme Court *Dred Scott* decision was wrong. The last proposition argued slavery was wrong.[8]

The **given** in the first proposition's **Enunciation** latched on to a Stephen A. Douglas sentence, "Our fathers, when they framed the Government under which we live, understood this question just as well, and even better, than we do now." Lincoln turned that Douglas assertion into an admission. It focused the **sought**:

> **Enunciation: [Given]** The facts with which I shall deal this evening are mainly old and familiar; nor is there anything new in the general use I shall make of them. If there shall be any novelty, it will be in the mode of presenting the facts, and the inferences and observations following that presentation. In his speech last autumn, at Columbus, Ohio, as reported in "The New-York Times," Senator Douglas said: "Our fathers, when they framed the Government under which we live, understood this question just as well, and even better, than we do now." I fully indorse this, and I adopt it as a text for this discourse. I so adopt it because it furnishes a precise and an agreed starting point for a discussion between Republicans and that wing of the Democracy headed by Senator Douglas. It simply leaves the inquiry: [**Sought**] "What was the understanding those fathers had of the question mentioned?"[9]

The **Exposition** framed the Investigation:

**Exposition:** What is the frame of Government under which we live?

The answer must be: "The Constitution of the United States." That Constitution consists of the original, framed in 1787, (and under which the present government first went into operation,) and twelve subsequently framed amendments, the first ten of which were framed in 1789.

Who were our fathers that framed the Constitution? I suppose the "thirty-nine" who signed the original instrument may be fairly called our fathers who framed that part of the present Government. It is almost exactly true to say they framed it, and it is altogether true to say they fairly represented the opinion and sentiment of the whole nation at that time. Their names, being familiar to nearly all, and accessible to quite all, need not now be repeated.

I take these "thirty-nine" for the present, as being "our fathers who framed the Government under which we live."[10]

The **Specification** refined the **sought**:

**Specification:** What is the question which, according to the text, those fathers understood "just as well, and even better than we do now?"

It is this: Does the proper division of local from federal authority, or anything in the Constitution, forbid our Federal Government to control as to slavery in our Federal Territories?

Upon this, Senator Douglas holds the affirmative, and Republicans the negative. This affirmation and denial form an issue; and this issue—this question—is precisely what the text declares our fathers understood "better than we."[11]

The **Construction** arrayed facts regarding Constitution signers' votes, to the extent they existed, on legislation related to the federal government's power to control slavery in the territories. The last sentence of the **Construction** was: "The cases I have mentioned are the only acts of the 'thirty-nine,' or of any of them, upon the direct issue, which I have been able to discover."[12]

The issue was reduced to what a majority of the founders thought regarding the power under the Constitution to forbid the federal government to control slavery in the territories.

The **Proof** argued federal constitutional authority to regulate slavery in the territories could be shown by the factual voting record of over 50% of the founders on legislation to control an aspect of slavery in the territories.

The oath of office founders took was central to the proposition. Beginning in 1789, Members of Congress took the oath, "I, A. B. do solemnly swear or affirm (as the case may be) that I will support the Constitution of the United States."[13] President Washington took a similar oath specified in the Constitution: "I do solemnly swear (or affirm) that I will faithfully execute the Office of President of the United States, and will to the best of my Ability, preserve, protect and defend the Constitution of the United States."[14]

Lincoln argued surely a signer of the United States Constitution would not violate his oath of office. Cooper Union's first proposition collected facts regarding signer votes or actions that appeared to regulate slavery in the territories. Most of those facts were arrayed in the **Construction**. Lincoln transformed the opposition's "admission" that the founders understood the question better than we, into a demonstration against Douglas's popular sovereignty position regarding introduction of slavery in the territories.[15]

A purpose of the Investigation is to acquire the facts or evidence necessary to form the **Specification's** proposed inference, or hypothesis. The Investigation also locates facts to array or marshal in the **Construction**. The **Construction** should not venture much beyond established facts.

Leveraged by what appeared to be indisputable logic,[16] the first proposition's **Construction** provided information regarding Constitution signers votes on federal legislation related to slavery in the territories. Lincoln presented signers' votes on six pieces of legislation:

Four signers of the Constitution - Congress of the Confederation voted to prohibit slavery in the Northwestern Territory in 1784.

Two signers of the Constitution - Congress of the Confederation voted into law the 1787 Northwest Ordinance.

Seventeen signers of the Constitution - Congress in 1789 passed an act to enforce the Northwest Ordinance, including George Washington signing the bill as President.

Three signers of the Constitution - Congress voted on organization of the Territory of Mississippi in 1798.

Two signers of the Constitution - Congress approved the Louisiana Purchase in 1804.

Two signers of the Constitution - Missouri Compromise question considered by Congress in 1819-1820, related to the expansion of slavery into the western territories.[17]

Facts arrayed in the **Construction** led to a long Proof that argued the logical consequences.

Proof or argument should reason scientifically. It should recite what follows as a matter of reasoning.[18] Because the Proof is set up by admitted or obvious facts, it should seem self-evident. Lincoln's Proof led to this articulated Lincoln **Conclusion**:

> The sum of the whole is, that of our thirty-nine fathers who framed the original Constitution, twenty-one—a clear majority of the whole—certainly understood that no proper division of local from federal authority, nor any part of the Constitution, forbade the Federal Government to control slavery in the federal territories; while all the rest probably had the same understanding. Such, unquestionably, was the understanding of our fathers who framed the original Constitution; and the text [Douglas' speech referenced in the **Given**] affirms that they understood the question "better than we."[19]

*If a proposition does not have an **Exposition**, is an Investigation still required?*

In general an **Exposition** is not required. Because a six element proposition tends to be more robust than a three, four, or five element proposition, it makes sense to use six elements in most, if not all, situations.

A proposition that does not have an **Exposition**, has at least a **given** and **sought** within its **Enunciation**, plus it has a Proof, and a **Conclusion**. An Investigation arguably is necessary to search out facts to reason scientifically within a Proof, and reach a **Conclusion**.

Even if there is an **Exposition**, performing the Investigation is not expressly required. An **Exposition** needs to add enough facts so that anyone who wants to investigate has facts necessary to support a proper Investigation.

*What is the argument that an Investigation is always required?*

An Investigation helps a writer or speaker to frame a proper **sought**, and reason scientifically to reach a sound **Conclusion**. Just as important, a properly framed proposition enables other people to test the proposition within its own terms.

*Under what circumstances should an **Exposition** be required in a proposition?*

If there are not enough facts in the **given**, and not enough specificity in the **sought** to know what to investigate, one can argue that an **Exposition** should be required. Proclus does not vocalize this.

William Herndon described what convinced Lincoln, and how Lincoln convinced others:

> Mr. Lincoln was a peculiar man, having a peculiar mind; he was gifted with a peculiarity, namely, a new look-out on nature. Everything had to be newly created for him—facts newly gathered, newly arranged, and newly classed. He had no faith, as already expressed. In order to believe he must see and feel, and thrust his hand into the place. He must taste, smell and handle before he had faith, *i.e.*, belief. Such a mind as this must act slowly, must have its time. His forte and power lay in his love of digging out for himself and hunting up for his own mind its own food, to be assimilated unto itself; and then in time he could and would form opinions and conclusions that no human power could overthrow. They were as irresistible as iron thunder, as powerful as logic embodied in mathematics.[20]

Perhaps Herndon described a language of science for human problems.[21]

## QUESTIONS

ONE: What makes mathematical logic powerful?

TWO: What makes the logic of plane geometry powerful?

THREE: What three elements are directly affected by the Investigation? How?

FOUR: What three elements are indirectly affected by the Investigation? How?

FIVE: From most influenced to least influenced, what is the order of the elements most affected by the Investigation?

SIX: Why isn't there a separate element called "Investigation?"

SEVEN: Why isn't the **Exposition** called "Investigation?"

EIGHT: What is the argument that an **Exposition** should always be required? This question becomes important when writing a three element proposition because an **Exposition** is not one of the three required elements.

# LESSON TWELVE

# WRITING

A six-element proposition's road to credibility is paved with facts. Investigate and know the facts. Accumulate "good" and "bad" facts. Facts that on the surface appear to refute a proposition are just as important as facts that support it. Put each on a 3 x 5 card, in a notebook, an electronic database, digital outliner, or in a combination of information containers. For Abraham Lincoln, that container could be his hat.[1]

Everything begins with facts and thoughts. The Investigation should reach a critical mass. Preparation moves to drafting. The **Enunciation** and **Exposition** should be drafted reasonably early.

It should not matter what element is worked on at any point in time. The **Specification** is a hypothesis. When you feel comfortable, one approach is to draft the **Specification** early. Get out of your own skin and honestly evaluate whether your **Specification** can be scientifically confirmed. If needed, revise the **Specification** to a more provable hypothesis.

When drafting the **Enunciation**, choose fundamental, necessary facts appropriate for the **given**. Trim, reorder, and rephrase facts in the **given** for a firm foundation. Draft the **sought**. The **sought** is more general and impartial than the **Specification**. The **given** and the **sought** complete the **Enunciation**.

Draft the **Exposition** with appropriate, non-argumentative facts. These largely indisputable facts combine with the **Enunciation** to enable the Investigation. Think about approaches to the Proof. After re-examining the **Specification**, array facts in the **Construction** that lead into the Proof. Avoid direct argument in the **Construction**.

Draft the Proof. Argument should be largely logic-based if the **Construction** was well developed. Argument may be a mixture of facts and logic. Reason scientifically.

Draft a **Conclusion** that clearly affirms what was proved or demonstrated.

Any change in the **Specification** will directly affect all, or most other elements. If the first four elements are carefully drafted, the Proof should flow; it should almost draft itself. The elements of a proposition make argument (Proof) easier.

Tailor phrasing and tone to the specific element. Tone builds credibility. Even though some elements are mostly fact, understand the elements as structural vessels of persuasive logic. Keep in mind the most important part of a demonstration is credibility. That is why the Investigation, which itself is not an element, is vital.

One strategy is start with a template, perhaps with three blank lines between each element. It can list the elements of a proposition (with definitions if needed) in a text processor, word processor, database, or outliner. To create a demonstration, fill in each element's content. The substance of each element need not initially be optimal. Put substance in the proper vessel, then refine. Make sure content flows smoothly. Revise and refine. Revise and refine.

Free-form databases designed for writing, like Scrivener[2] (available on Macs and PCs) can be used in addition to text processors and word processors.

Outliners are powerful. Some electronic outliners are free; others are moderately priced; some are expensive. Use what is comfortable. Dedicated outliners are generally better than word processor outliners. Text processors and word processors are fine for finishing and polishing a writing that started in an outliner.

An outliner can have a separate heading for each of the six elements. The **Enunciation** should have two subsections: a **given** and a **sought**. Move sentences and paragraphs into the element they fit. Order statements within each element. Revise and refine as needed. An outliner's beauty includes the ability to collapse, expand, focus, and move hierarchically. Content can be quickly ordered, reordered, and edited.

The Gettysburg Address in outline form:

**1. Enunciation**
    A. **Given**
        1) Four score and seven years ago our fathers brought forth on this continent, a new nation, conceived in Liberty,
        2) and dedicated to the proposition that all men are created equal.
        3) Now we are engaged in a great civil war,
    B. **Sought** - testing whether that nation, or any nation so conceived and so dedicated, can long endure.
**2. Exposition** - We are met on a great battle-field of that war.

## 3. Specification

A. We have come to dedicate a portion of that field, as a final resting place for those who here gave their lives that that nation might live.

B. It is altogether fitting and proper that we should do this.

## 4. Construction

A. But, in a larger sense, we can not dedicate—we can not consecrate—we can not hallow—this ground. The brave men, living and dead, who struggled here, have consecrated it, far above our poor power to add or detract.

B. The world will little note, nor long remember what we say here,

C. but it can never forget what they did here.

## 5. Proof

A. It is for us the living, rather, to be dedicated here to the unfinished work which they who fought here have thus far so nobly advanced.

B. It is rather for us to be here dedicated to the great task remaining before us

C. —that from these honored dead we take increased devotion to that cause for which they gave the last full measure of devotion

D. —that we here highly resolve that these dead shall not have died in vain

## 6. Conclusion

A. —that this nation, under God, shall have a new birth of freedom

B. —and that government of the people, by the people, for the people, shall not perish from the earth.

Another technique is to compose on a blank sheet of paper, or on a blank screen. Draft patiently, thoughtfully, and honestly. Don't forget Abraham Lincoln's habit of writing fragments (akin to 3 x 5 cards) that can be sorted into elements, then reordered within particular elements. Use and develop comfortable composition tools and habits.

## PERSUASIVE COMPOSITION

**Enunciation**: [**Given**] Two sets of compatible tools optimize persuasive composition, one new and one ancient. The new is digital, and largely mechanical; the ancient is theoretical. The new focuses on easy information management. The ancient is the six elements of a proposition. The elements methodically form a demonstration. [**Sought**] Both sets of tools are desirable.

**Exposition**: At some point research needs a digital aspect. The more sophisticated and thorough the research, the more necessary digital organization. Use whatever digital tools you find comfortable.

**Specification**: Internalize the ancient persuasive structure of the six elements of a proposition. Use comfortable digital tools.

**Construction**: Raw information, ideally from primary sources, needs to be stored. Composition also needs, but does not necessarily require, modern tools. An outliner may be a useful composition tool. A free form database like Scrivener, which essentially is an outliner with the muscle of a database, can be a powerful digital composition tool if it suits you. Text processors work for many. Pencil and paper may suffice.

**Proof**: The six elements structure a persuasive end product. The elements are worth internalizing. Work to become comfortable with the elements and with digital tools to optimize persuasive product.

**Conclusion**: The backbone of a persuasive six-element demonstration includes hard work, facts, and scientific reasoning. Ancient theory and modern tools enhance composition within six-element structure.

## QUESTIONS

ONE: What makes the six elements easy to use?

TWO: What makes the six elements difficult to use?

THREE: What is the best way to become proficient with the six elements of a proposition?

# GENERAL PRINCIPLES

When composing a demonstration, consider:

1. Is the proposition (the demonstration) weighted more in fact than argument? It ideally should be.
2. Will the listener or reader become a partner in the search for the truth, and naturally anticipate what is coming?
3. Is appropriate respect shown for opposing views?
4. Do you understand the argument against the proposition as well as you understand the argument for it?
5. Are you aware of the three weakest points in your argument?
6. How would you attack your own proposition?
7. How would you defend your proposition's most vulnerable points?

*Are there unnecessary statements in the demonstration?* The relatively lengthy Declaration of Independence is thorough, yet tight (Lesson 16). The Gettysburg Address does not waste a syllable. While everything necessary should be there, nothing unnecessary should appear. A proposition structured according to the six elements naturally focuses. **Enunciation**, **Exposition**, **Specification**, **Construction**, **Proof**, and **Conclusion** define purpose and provide location.

*Are there words within an element that do not serve the element's purpose?* They should be cut, changed, or moved. This rule is not absolute. At the minimum, be aware (and beware) of content that strays from an element's purpose.

*Are necessary statements missing; are there gaps in the demonstration?* Do you prove, or demonstrate, what you set out to? A well-constructed proposition has no factual gaps, and no logical gaps. Facts lay the groundwork for the **Proof**'s argument.

After tightly marshaled factual evidence arrayed in its **Construction**, the Declaration of Independence **Proof** solidly argued for political separation. Jefferson's **Proof** used past tense verbs. The American colonies "warned," "reminded," "appealed," and "conjured." The **Conclusion** articulated separation from Great Britain. The Declaration (Lesson 16) was a detailed, straightforward, six-element masterpiece.

In the Gettysburg Address, a cemetery dedication artfully focused 272 words on national survival. Its **Proof** looked to the future. Abraham Lincoln argued action that must be taken to preserve the Union: "be dedicated," "be here dedicated," "take increased devotion," and "highly resolve." The Address was a call to action to assure the Union's survival. Its **Conclusion** stated, "…government of the people, by the people, for the people, shall not perish from the earth." With inspirational completeness within six-element logic, Lincoln presented a three minute demonstration of national survival.

*Is the presentation gimmick free, yet artful? Is attention maintained?* Abraham Lincoln's Springfield Farewell Address (Lesson 10) leveraged 152 words. The **sought** was "parting." The **Specification** described an uncertain parting. The **Construction** summarized Lincoln's challenge: "…with a task before me greater than that which rested upon Washington." The **Proof** argued what was needed for a positive result. In the **Conclusion**, the **sought's** "parting," and the **Specification's** uncertain parting, became "an affectionate farewell" with mutual prayer to deal with the future's uncertainty.

*Is the angle of "attack" interesting?* Abraham Lincoln's March 4, 1865, Second Inaugural proposition (Lesson 16) was both interesting and controversial. It concluded:

> With malice toward none; with charity for all; with firmness in the right, as God gives us to see the right, let us strive on to finish the work we are in; to bind up the nation's wounds; to care for him who shall have borne the battle, and for his widow, and his orphan—to do all which may achieve and cherish a just, and a lasting peace, among ourselves, and with all nations.[1]

With the Civil War almost over, Abraham Lincoln knew the Second Inaugural's reasoning might not be popular. A March 15, 1865, letter stated, "I expect the latter [the Second Inaugural] to wear as well as—perhaps better than—any thing I have produced; but I believe it is not immediately popular."[2]

On January 9, 1814, Thomas Jefferson wrote two similar letters to different people. The propositions were nearly identical. Jefferson used three elements in one letter (Pintard), and six elements in the other (Burnside). Note the additional texture in the six-element letter to Samuel M. Burnside. Compare it to the less robust letter to Pintard.

## To John Pintard

Sir                                    Monticello Jan. 9. 14.[3]
**Enunciation:** [**Given**] I have duly recieved your favor of Dec. 22. informing me that the New York Historical society had been pleased to elect me an honorary member of that institution. I am entirely sensible of the honor done me by this election; [**Sought**] and I pray you to become the channel of my grateful acknolegments to the society.

**Proof:** at this distance, and at my time of life, I cannot but be conscious how little it will be in my power to further their views: but I shall certainly, and with great pleasure, embrace any occasion which shall occur of rendering them any services in my power.

**Conclusion:** with these assurances be so good as to accept for them and for yourself those of my high respect and consideration.
                                            Th: Jefferson

## To Samuel M. Burnside

Sir                                    Monticello. Jan. 9. 1814.[4]
**Enunciation:** [**Given**] I have duly recieved your favor of the 13th of December, informing me of the institution of the American Antiquarian Society [**Sought**] and expressing it's disposition to honor me with an admission into it, and the request of my cooperation in the advancement of it's objects.

**Exposition:** no one can be more sensible of the honor and the favor of these dispositions,

**Specification:** and I pray you to have the goodness to testify to them all the gratitude I feel on recieving assurances of them.

**Construction:** there has been a time of life when I should have entered into their views with zeal, and with a hope of not being altogether unuseful.

**Proof:** but, now more than Septagenary, retired from the active scenes and business of life, I am sensible how little I can contribute to the advancement of the objects of their establishment; and that I should be but an unprofitable member, carrying into the institution indeed my best wishes for it's success, and a readiness to serve it on any occasion which should occur.

**Conclusion:** with these acknolegements, be so good as to accept, for the society as well as for yourself the assurances of my high respect & consideration.

Th: Jefferson

## FACTS FEED THE FORCE OF REASON

**Enunciation**: [**Given**] Thorough investigation of reasonably framed facts form the foundation of six-element demonstration. Facts should be firm, not manipulative tools of crowd-pleasing sizzle. [**Sought**] Believe nothing; confirm everything.

**Exposition**: Facts are truth. Location within a demonstration is timing. Logical force is a vector of scientific reasoning.

**Specification**: Leadership requires credibility and the ability to demonstrate.

**Construction**: A true leader can make a difficult proposition self-evident.

**Proof**: Facts are visible weapons. Credibility can be an invisible weapon.

**Conclusion**: The logical force of reason is irresistible when facts properly combine with credibility meshed with scientific reasoning.

## QUESTIONS

ONE: What are the three most important general principles in Lesson 13? Why?

TWO: What three general principles in Lesson 13 best highlight artful use of the elements in the Gettysburg Address? Explain.

THREE: What is the power of location within a six element proposition? How does it operate?

FOUR: What is the definition of credibility?

FIVE: What gives a six-element proposition more texture and robustness than a three element proposition on the same topic? How?

# CREDIBILITY IS EVERYTHING

The location and substance of every word, sentence, and paragraph should be designed to increase credibility. Thomas Jefferson addressed the issue of a perpetual motion machine described in a November 30, 1812, letter from Robert Patterson. December 27, 1812, he wrote Patterson (Lesson 17).

The **sought** established Jefferson's skepticism: "I had never before been able to form an idea of what his principle of deception was." Jefferson's **Exposition** described the machine as "…amusing them [observers] with a sham machinery…" The **Specification** characterized the machine as "…a more extensive delusion than I have before witnessed on this point." The **Proof** argued "…the equilibrium established by him between cause & effect must be suspended to effect that purpose." Annoyed by misquotation, Jefferson forcefully made his points without letting his annoyance interfere. He relentlessly attacked the sham of perpetual motion.

Despite the fairly obvious fact perpetual motion machines are preposterous, Jefferson's demonstration was weak to the extent it relied on his pre-existing credibility. In effect, Jefferson called the machine's inventor a liar. Compare this to Abraham Lincoln's argument to Stephen A. Douglas in the Lincoln-Douglas Debates: "Now, if you undertake to disprove that [plane geometry] proposition, and to show that it is erroneous, would you prove it to be false by calling Euclid a liar?"[1]

Well before *The Wizard of Oz*, the perpetual motion machine's "principle of deception" was a hidden person turning a crank.[2] Credibility is everything.

*Is the listener or reader naturally going to anticipate what is coming; is the listener or reader a partner in the search for the truth?* The **sought** and **Specification** (hypothesis) can function like a riddle to be solved. A six-element proposition tells a story. The texture and timing of the six elements naturally do this logically. Factual detail and straight forward reasoning make it easy to anticipate the Declaration of Independence **Proof** (Lesson 16, pages 120-121).

It is important to engage the audience as a partner in the search for truth. The six elements do this well. Assuming a solid proposition, there is rarely anything more persuasive to a listener or reader than to anticipate a sound **Proof** and **Conclusion** before they are articulated. The listener or reader then owns it.

President Lincoln's Second Inaugural Address (Lesson 16) led the audience to its **Conclusion**. The **Exposition** pushed factual background. The **Construction** presented basic, on point facts: "Both read the same Bible, and pray to the same God; and each invokes His aid against the other." The **Proof** used these basic facts to argue slavery was an "offence" for North and South. This led to a **Conclusion** that called for reconciliation, not revenge.

The Gettysburg Address flows, with sophisticated focus on a precise goal. Those who heard Lincoln deliver the Address, or read it later, probably felt a partnership with him in the search for truth. Like many Lincoln speeches, even long ones, the Gettysburg Address was printed in newspapers.[3] Two-thirds of metropolitan Republican newspapers printed the Gettysburg Address on page one.[4]

*Is the proposition or demonstration more fact based than argument based?* With proper facts, the first draft of an argument nearly writes itself. Without facts, credibility wants. The **given** in President Barack Obama's May 1, 2011, speech announced Osama bin Laden's death (Lesson 17). It presented facts related to September 11, 2001, including Osama bin Laden's link to al Qaeda. At the time the speech was broadcast, the President largely relied on his own credibility for the core statement that bin Laden was dead. The **Exposition** presented facts related to the 10-year search for Osama bin Laden. The **Construction** presented facts related to the mission that killed Osama bin Laden. The **Proof** built from these facts. It argued the battle against al Qaeda needed to continue. The **Conclusion** gave thanks justice was done. There was no objective factual confirmation in the speech of bin Laden's death.

The Declaration of Independence (Lesson 16) is a detailed fact-based demonstration. Its main purpose was to enhance the likelihood of the Revolutionary War's success by convincing Americans to support war, and foreigners to support American independence.

In the Gettysburg Address, Abraham Lincoln argued what must happen for the United States to survive. The Gettysburg Address used fewer facts than the Declaration. The facts in the Gettysburg Address were high level. Facts were complicated by the uncertainties of the Civil War. The **Proof** bootstrapped aspirational facts. It spoke about likely victory, but did not take victory for granted. Lincoln argued action was still required.

*Is appropriate respect shown for those with an opposing view?* Credibility and civility are related. The six elements foster civility. Though not a substitute for facts, civility aids credibility almost as much as facts. A basis of civility is presumptive recognition that those with an opposing view are sincere in their belief. Civility makes persuasion more likely. That does not imply moral equivalence. While there are examples of seemingly pure evil in human history, too often human debate is framed as a battle between good and evil. It becomes easy for vicious adjectives and naked conclusions to dominate, rather than facts and scientific reasoning. A proposition constructed within the six elements promotes civil discourse by channeling factual focus and logical purity to a clean, scientifically reasoned, **Conclusion**.

A quick way to make an audience uncomfortable is to personally attack an opponent. An audience usually punishes the person conducting a personal attack. Notice Abraham Lincoln's civility while taking down Stephen A. Douglas. In 1858, Lincoln was a candidate for the United States Senate. On June 16, 1858, he delivered his "House Divided" speech at the Republican state convention in Springfield, Illinois. Lincoln argued, "I believe this government cannot endure, permanently half <u>slave</u> and half <u>free</u>."

> Now, as ever, I wish to not <u>misrepresent</u> Judge Douglas' <u>position</u>, question his <u>motives</u>, or do ought that can be personally offensive to him. Whenever, <u>if ever</u>, he and we can come together on <u>principle</u> so that <u>our great cause</u> may have assistance from <u>his great ability</u>, I hope to have interposed no adventitious obstacle. But clearly, he is not <u>now</u> with us—he does not <u>pretend</u> to be—he does not <u>promise</u> to <u>ever</u> be...[5]

After pointedly, but factually, describing positions of his opponent Stephen A. Douglas, Lincoln's **Conclusion** was forceful yet civil.

The Declaration of Independence (Lesson 16) presented facts that showed patient colonies and despotic colonial authority. The six elements enabled channeled expression and focused passion. Emotion, if not totally subdued, was controlled. The Declaration of Independence dutifully presented fact after fact. Though Great Britain challenged the facts, it almost seemed there could not be a counter argument. If the war's outcome seemed uncertain in 1776, its necessity did not.

*Are you aware of the three weakest points in your argument; how would you attack your own proposition; how would you defend its three most vulnerable points?* Keep in mind your weak points (or weakest points). Constantly refine your thought. Lincoln's view of slavery developed. One can start with the October 16, 1854, Peoria speech,[6] the June 16, 1858, House Divided speech,[7] and go through the February 27, 1860, address at Cooper Institute,[8] the March 4, 1861, First Inaugural

Address,[9] then the March 4, 1865, Second Inaugural Address (Lesson 16). Almost every Lincoln speech that touched on slavery, refined earlier arguments.

## STRENGTH AND VULNERABILITY

**Enunciation**: [**Given**] A six element demonstration should be more fact based than argument based. [**Sought**] Understand your weak points better than your strong points.

**Exposition**: Generally respect should be shown for the opposition.

**Specification**: Know your greatest vulnerabilities. Then eliminate them.

**Construction**: Ideally a listener or reader will naturally anticipate what is coming as though a partner in the search for the truth.

**Proof**: Everything builds around what is necessary to your demonstration. Nothing more. Nothing less. Be artful without gimmicks. Vulnerability can be minimized by additional facts, or an adjusted **Specification**, or a shifted argument.

**Conclusion**: Understanding your weak points frees you to emphasize your strong points. The **Specification** controls the **Proof**. How the battle is chosen controls its outcome.

## QUESTIONS

ONE: What are the two most important general principles in Lesson 14? Why?

TWO: Which principles in Lesson 14 best highlight artful use of the elements in the Gettysburg Address? Explain.

# COLLABORATE

Creation of a six-element persuasive demonstration is like solving a puzzle. Collaboration is group puzzle-solving. The six elements make group puzzle-solving easier. A committee or team formed with the six elements in mind can elegantly divide work and combine effort.

For instance, a well–staffed team may want two groups that work independently. The same **Specification** may be assigned. In some instances the same **sought** could be assigned. Ultimately one draft or the other can be chosen, or the drafts can be blended.

There is room for art within a six-element proposition. Element definitions set the parameters. Location based elements orchestrate word choice, sentence tone, and paragraph function. Creativity can blossom within methodical structure. Because six-element structure provides solid location within six vessels for language, creativity is easier. The elements self-enforce structure for team creation of persuasive verbal or written demonstrations based on facts and scientific reasoning.

Sometimes a proposition's hypothesis is predetermined, assigned, or dictated by the situation. Work on a proposition begins with factual investigation and analysis. If the specific topic is known, factual investigation can be immediately delegated. If the topic is open, at least a general area should be obvious; some investigation can begin before determination of the **sought** and **Specification**.

Once facts on both sides of a proposition are known, the team needs to sort and analyze. The elements dynamically push facts to their logical location. A fact-based **given**, plus a general and neutral **sought**, form the **Enunciation**. A fact-based **Exposition** pushes an Investigation toward needed facts that are directly or indirectly useful in the last four elements. For instance, the **Specification** is a hypothesis that is framed within the limits of known applicable facts. A largely fact-based **Construction** anchors truth within arrayed evidence. Perfectly timed scientific reasoning in the **Proof** leads to a **Conclusion** that becomes fact. Elements control timing and tone.

If there is an early sense of a probable **Specification**, the **Enunciation** and the **Exposition** may easily fall into place. The Investigation eases the way to a

**Specification**, **Construction**, and **Proof** that properly mesh. The **Enunciation** (which builds toward the **Exposition**) can be adjusted to fit the outer limits of the Investigation. As everything lines up, synergies coalesce.

A proposition flows by logical development from the **Enunciation's** high level **sought**, into a narrowed **Specification**, to the **Conclusion's** clear statement of what was proved. Facts wrap around logical development from **sought**, to **Specification**, to **Conclusion**. The nature of the six elements is textured simplicity based on structural location. Structure provides vessels of credibility.

Six-element structure helps drafts maintain proper tone and focus. For instance, "And the war came" in the **Exposition** of Abraham Lincoln's Second Inaugural (Lesson 16, page 131), naturally fits where it is. Because of the six elements, it does not take genius or restraint to choose a clean, non-argumentative, factual phrase made beautiful by the natural purpose of its location. In the Gettysburg Address, the **Exposition** is, "We are met on a great battle-field of that war."

No slick tricks or gimmicks. Six-element, structural vessels engineer natural functionality. Locational purpose among the vessels of the six elements frees time for penetrating elegance. Expression is naturally substantive, and persuasive. Fact research, brainstorming, drafting, refining, editing, and polishing are enhanced by skilled team members. A six-element collaborative environment ideally leads to better analysis, better decisions, and quicker composition of persuasive demonstrations.

## QUESTIONS

ONE: How do the six elements make collaboration easier?

TWO: What is the best way to use the six elements collaboratively?

THREE: How can a solo author compensate for the lack of "person power" in the composition of six element propositions?

FOUR: What are the drawbacks of collaborative composition of a proposition?

# LESSON SIXTEEN

# FREEDOM

16.1 The Declaration of Independence

16.2 The Virginia Statute for Religious Freedom

16.3 Abraham Lincoln's Address at Cooper Institute, First Proposition

16.4 Abraham Lincoln's Second Inaugural Address

This lesson presents two Thomas Jefferson writings, and two Abraham Lincoln writings.

## 16.1 THE DECLARATION OF INDEPENDENCE

Ohio Judge R. M. Wanamaker wrote in 1918:

> Where did he [Lincoln] get this order which he habitually followed in his discussions on law or government? He does not definitely advise us. Neither do any of his biographers. It is, however, more than passing strange that Lincoln's early acquaintance with, and study of, the Declaration of Independence brought him directly and intimately in touch with this method of presentation and argument. That Declaration of Independence is naturally divisible into those same three parts, declaration, demonstration, dedication. It is most natural for us to presume that Lincoln, who studied and quoted the Declaration of Independence more frequently than any other American statesman of his own time, or any other, should have been strikingly impressed with the logical order so plainly and powerfully put in the Declaration of Independence, by his great prototype, Thomas Jefferson.[1]

Historian Dumas Malone's 1954 view of the Declaration of Independence:

> THE PAPER that had been adopted by Congress and proclaimed from Georgia to New Hampshire can be roughly divided into four parts: a preamble, a philosophical paragraph, a list of charges against the King, and at the end the actual declaration of independence—including the resolution adopted on July 2.[2]

While Wanamaker and Malone did not see the Declaration's actual structure, it is to their credit that they looked for it.

**IN CONGRESS, July 4, 1776.**[3]

THE UNANIMOUS DECLARATION of the thirteen united STATES OF AMERICA,

ENUNCIATION: [**Given**] When in the Course of human events, it becomes necessary for one people to dissolve the political bands which have connected them with another, and to assume among the powers of the earth, the separate and equal station to which the Laws of Nature and of Nature's God entitle them, a decent respect to the opinions of mankind requires that [**Sought**] they should declare the causes which impel them to the separation.

EXPOSITION: We hold these truths to be self-evident, that all men are created equal, that they are endowed by their Creator with certain unalienable Rights, that among these are Life, Liberty and the pursuit of Happiness.

That to secure these rights, Governments are instituted among Men, deriving their just powers from the consent of the governed,

That whenever any Form of Government becomes destructive of these ends, it is the Right of the People to alter or to abolish it, and to institute new Government, laying its foundation on such principles and organizing its powers in such form, as to them shall seem most likely to effect their Safety and Happiness.

Prudence, indeed, will dictate that Governments long established should not be changed for light and transient causes; and accordingly all experience hath shewn, that mankind are more disposed to suffer, while evils are sufferable, than to right themselves by abolishing the forms to which they are accustomed.

SPECIFICATION: But when a long train of abuses and usurpations, pursuing invariably the same Object evinces a design to reduce them under absolute Despotism, it is their right, it is their duty, to throw off such Government, and to provide new Guards for their future security. Such has been the patient sufferance of these Colonies; and such is now the necessity which constrains them to alter their former Systems of Government.

CONSTRUCTION: The history of the present King of Great Britain is a history of repeated injuries and usurpations, all having in direct object the establishment of an absolute Tyranny over these States. To prove this, let Facts be submitted to a candid world.

He has refused his Assent to Laws, the most wholesome and necessary for the public good.

He has forbidden his Governors to pass Laws of immediate and pressing importance, unless suspended in their operation till his Assent should be obtained; and when so suspended, he has utterly neglected to attend to them.

He has refused to pass other Laws for the accommodation of large districts of people, unless those people would relinquish the right of Representation in the Legislature, a right inestimable to them and formidable to tyrants only.

He has called together legislative bodies at places unusual, uncomfortable, and distant from the depository of their public Records, for the sole purpose of fatiguing them into compliance with his measures.

He has dissolved Representative Houses repeatedly, for opposing with manly firmness his invasions on the rights of the people.

He has refused for a long time, after such dissolutions, to cause others to be elected; whereby the Legislative powers, incapable of Annihilation, have returned to the People at large for their exercise; the State remaining in the mean time exposed to all the dangers of invasion from without, and convulsions within.

He has endeavoured to prevent the population of these States; for that purpose obstructing the Laws for Naturalization of Foreigners; refusing to pass others to encourage their migrations hither, and raising the conditions of new Appropriations of Lands.

He has obstructed the Administration of Justice, by refusing his Assent to Laws for establishing Judiciary powers.

He has made Judges dependent on his Will alone, for the tenure of their offices, and the amount and payment of their salaries.

He has erected a multitude of New Offices, and sent hither swarms of Officers to harrass our people, and eat out their substance.

He has kept among us, in times of peace, standing Armies without the Consent of our legislatures.

He has affected to render the Military independent of and superior to the Civil power.

He has combined with others to subject us to a jurisdiction foreign to our constitution, and unacknowledged by our laws; giving his Assent to their Acts of pretended Legislation:

For Quartering large bodies of armed troops among us:

For protecting them, by a mock Trial, from punishment for any Murders which they should commit on the Inhabitants of these States:

For cutting off our Trade with all parts of the world:

For imposing Taxes on us without our Consent:

For depriving us in many cases of the benefits of Trial by Jury:

For transporting us beyond Seas to be tried for pretended offences:

For abolishing the free System of English Laws in a neighbouring Province, establishing therein an Arbitrary government, and enlarging its Boundaries so as to render it at once an example and fit instrument for introducing the same absolute rule into these Colonies:

For taking away our Charters, abolishing our most valuable Laws, and altering fundamentally the Forms of our Governments:

For suspending our own Legislatures, and declaring themselves invested with power to legislate for us in all cases whatsoever.

He has abdicated Government here, by declaring us out of his Protection and waging War against us.

He has plundered our seas, ravaged our Coasts, burnt our towns, and destroyed the Lives of our people.

He is at this time transporting large Armies of foreign Mercenaries to compleat the works of death, desolation and tyranny, already begun with circumstances of Cruelty & perfidy scarcely paralleled in the most barbarous ages, and totally unworthy the Head of a civilized nation.

He has constrained our fellow Citizens taken Captive on the high Seas to bear Arms against their Country, to become the executioners of their friends and Brethren, or to fall themselves by their Hands.

He has excited domestic insurrections amongst us, and has endeavoured to bring on the inhabitants of our frontiers, the merciless Indian Savages, whose known rule of warfare, is an undistinguished destruction of all ages, sexes and conditions.

**PROOF:** In every stage of these Oppressions We have Petitioned for Redress in the most humble terms:

Our repeated Petitions have been answered only by repeated injury. A Prince, whose character is thus marked by every act which may define a Tyrant, is unfit to be the ruler of a free people.

Nor have We been wanting in attentions to our Brittish brethren. We have warned them from time to time of attempts by their legislature to extend an unwarrantable jurisdiction over us. We have reminded them of the circumstances of our emigration and settlement here. We have appealed to their native justice and magnanimity, and we have conjured them by the ties of our common kindred to disavow these usurpations, which, would inevitably interrupt our connections and correspondence.

They too have been deaf to the voice of justice and of consanguinity. We must, therefore, acquiesce in the necessity, which denounces our Separation, and hold them, as we hold the rest of mankind, Enemies in War, in Peace Friends.

**CONCLUSION:** We, therefore, the Representatives of the united States of America, in General Congress, Assembled, appealing to the Supreme Judge of the world for the rectitude of our intentions, do, in the Name, and by Authority of the good People of these Colonies, solemnly publish and declare, That these United Colonies are, and of Right ought to be Free and Independent States; that they are Absolved from all Allegiance to the British Crown, and that all political connection between them and the State of Great Britain, is and ought to be totally dissolved;

and that as Free and Independent States, they have full Power to levy War, conclude Peace, contract Alliances, establish Commerce, and to do all other Acts and Things which Independent States may of right do. And for the support of this Declaration, with a firm reliance on the protection of divine Providence, we mutually pledge to each other our Lives, our Fortunes and our sacred Honor.

## 16.2 THE VIRGINIA STATUTE FOR RELIGIOUS FREEDOM

**ENUNCIATION:** [**Given**] <u>Well aware that the opinions and belief of men depend not on their own will, but follow involuntarily the evidence proposed to their minds</u>; [**Sought**] <u>that</u> Almighty God hath created the mind free, <u>and manifested his supreme will that free it shall remain by making it altogether insusceptible of restraint;</u>

**EXPOSITION:** that all attempts to influence it by temporal punishments, or burthens, or by civil incapacitations, tend only to beget habits of hypocrisy and meanness,

**SPECIFICATION:** and are a departure from the plan of the holy author of our religion, who being lord both of body and mind, yet chose not to propagate it by coercions on either, as was in his Almighty power to do, <u>but to extend it by its influence on reason alone;</u>

**CONSTRUCTION:** that the impious presumption of legislators and rulers, civil as well as ecclesiastical, who, being themselves but fallible and uninspired men, have assumed dominion over the faith of others, setting up their own opinions and modes of thinking as the only true and infallible, and as such endeavoring to impose them on others, hath established and maintained false religions over the greatest part of the world and through all time:

**PROOF:** That to compel a man to furnish contributions of money for the propagation of opinions which he disbelieves <u>and abhors</u>, is sinful and tyrannical;

that even the forcing him to support this or that teacher of his own religious persuasion, is depriving him of the comfortable liberty of giving his contributions to the particular pastor whose morals he would make his pattern, and whose powers he feels most persuasive to righteousness;

and is withdrawing from the ministry those temporary rewards, which proceeding from an approbation of their personal conduct, are an additional incitement to earnest and unremitting labours for the instruction of mankind;

that our civil rights have no dependance on our religious opinions, any more than our opinions in physics or geometry;

that therefore the proscribing any citizen as unworthy the public confidence by laying upon him an incapacity of being called to offices of trust and emolument, unless he profess or renounce this or that religious opinion, is depriving him injuriously of those privileges and advantages to which, in common with his fellow citizens, he has a natural right;

that it tends also to corrupt the principles of that <u>very</u> religion it is meant to encourage, by bribing, with a monopoly of worldly honours and emoluments, those who will externally profess and conform to it;

that though indeed these are criminal who do not withstand such temptation, yet neither are those innocent who lay the bait in their way;

<u>that the opinions of men are not the object of civil government, nor under its jurisdiction;</u>

that to suffer the civil magistrate to intrude his powers into the field of opinion and to restrain the profession or propagation of principles on supposition of their ill tendency is a dangerous falacy, which at once destroys all religious liberty, because he being of course judge of that tendency will make his opinions the rule of judgment, and approve or condemn the sentiments of others only as they shall square with or differ from his own;

that it is time enough for the rightful purposes of civil government for its officers to interfere when principles break out into overt acts against peace and good order;

and finally, that truth is great and will prevail if left to herself;

that she is the proper and sufficient antagonist to error, and has nothing to fear from the conflict unless by human interposition disarmed of her natural weapons, free argument and debate;

errors ceasing to be dangerous when it is permitted freely to contradict them.

**CONCLUSION:** <u>We the General Assembly of Virginia do enact</u> that no man shall be compelled to frequent or support any religious worship, place, or ministry whatsoever, nor shall be enforced, restrained, molested, or burthened in his body or goods, nor shall otherwise suffer, on account of his religious opinions or belief;

but that all men shall be free to profess, and by argument to maintain, their opinions in matters of religion, and that the same shall in no wise diminish, enlarge, or affect their civil capacities.

And though we well know that this Assembly, elected by the people for the ordinary purposes of legislation only, have no power to restrain the acts of succeeding Assemblies, constituted with powers equal to our own, and that therefore to declare this act irrevocable would be of no effect in law; yet we are free to declare, and do declare, that the rights hereby asserted are of the natural rights of mankind, and that if any act shall be hereafter passed to repeal the present or to narrow its operation, such act will be an infringement of natural right.[4]

*Paraphrased:*

**Enunciation:** [**Given**] Truth is absolute. [**Sought**] The human mind should not and cannot be forced into any particular belief system.

**Exposition:** Influence by force begets hypocrisy and meanness.

**Specification:** Religion should not be propagated by coercion; it should be extended by reason alone.

**Construction:** Religions differ on fundamental principles and therefore cannot be trusted to be infallible, particularly when forced on others.

**Proof:** Civil rights are inherent and absolute. Physics and geometry are absolute truth. Free thinking is a natural right. Force does not work. It is not for the government to define truth. Truth is not the business of government. Truth wins in an unfettered marketplace.

**Conclusion:** The government shall not force religious opinion on anyone. The marketplace of ideas will determine truth as a result of free expression. Freedom of opinion and expression are natural rights.

By drafting the Virginia Statute for Religious Freedom in the form of a "singular proposition," Jefferson cleverly forced those who voted on the statute to read the argument for its enactment. He wrote in his autobiography:

> The bill for establishing religious freedom, the principles of which had, to a certain degree, been enacted before, I had drawn in all the latitude of reason & right. it still met with opposition; but, with some mutilations in the preamble, it was finally past; and a singular proposition proved that it's protection of opinion was meant to be universal.[5]

## 16.3 ABRAHAM LINCOLN'S ADDRESS AT COOPER INSTITUTE
### FIRST PROPOSITION - FEBRUARY 27, 1860

MR. PRESIDENT AND FELLOW CITIZENS OF NEW YORK:

ENUNCIATION: [Given] —The facts with which I shall deal this evening are mainly old and familiar; nor is there anything new in the general use I shall make of them. If there shall be any novelty, it will be in the mode of presenting the facts, and the inferences and observations following that presentation.

In his speech last autumn, at Columbus, Ohio, as reported in "The New-York Times," Senator Douglas said:

"Our fathers, when they framed the Government under which we live, understood this question just as well, and even better, than we do now."

I fully indorse this, and I adopt it as a text for this discourse. I so adopt it because it furnishes a precise and an agreed starting point for a discussion between Republicans and that wing of the Democracy headed by Senator Douglas. It simply leaves the inquiry: [Sought] "What was the understanding those fathers had of the question mentioned?"

EXPOSITION: What is the frame of Government under which we live?

The answer must be: "The Constitution of the United States." That Constitution consists of the original, framed in 1787, (and under which the present government first went into operation,) and twelve subsequently framed amendments, the first ten of which were framed in 1789.

Who were our fathers that framed the Constitution? I suppose the "thirty-nine" who signed the original instrument may be fairly called our fathers who framed that part of the present Government. It is almost exactly true to say they framed it, and it is altogether true to say they fairly represented the opinion and sentiment of the whole nation at that time. Their names, being familiar to nearly all, and accessible to quite all, need not now be repeated.

I take these "thirty-nine" for the present, as being "our fathers who framed the Government under which we live."

SPECIFICATION: What is the question which, according to the text, those fathers understood "just as well, and even better than we do now?"

It is this: Does the proper division of local from federal authority, or anything in the Constitution, forbid <u>our Federal Government</u> to control as to slavery in <u>our Federal Territories</u>?

Upon this, Senator Douglas holds the affirmative, and Republicans the negative. This affirmation and denial form an issue; and this issue—this question—is precisely what the text declares our fathers understood "better than we."

**CONSTRUCTION:** Let us now inquire whether the "thirty-nine," or any of them, ever acted upon this question; and if they did, how they acted upon it—how they expressed that better understanding?

In 1784, three years before the Constitution—the United States then owning the Northwestern Territory, and no other, the Congress of the Confederation had before them the question of prohibiting slavery in that Territory; and four of the "thirty-nine" who afterward framed the Constitution, were in that Congress, and voted on that question. Of these, Roger Sherman, Thomas Mifflin, and Hugh Williamson voted for the prohibition, thus showing that, in their understanding, no line dividing local from federal authority, nor anything else, properly forbade the Federal Government to control as to slavery in federal territory. The other of the four—James M'Henry—voted against the prohibition, showing that, for some cause, he thought it improper to vote for it.

In 1787, still before the Constitution, but while the Convention was in session framing it, and while the Northwestern Territory still was the only territory owned by the United States, the same question of prohibiting slavery in the territory again came before the Congress of the Confederation; and two more of the "thirty-nine" who afterward signed the Constitution, were in that Congress, and voted on the question. They were William Blount and William Few; and they both voted for the prohibition—thus showing that, in their understanding, no line dividing local from federal authority, nor anything else, properly forbade the Federal Government to control as to slavery in federal territory. This time the prohibition became a law, being part of what is now well known as the Ordinance of '87.

The question of federal control of slavery in the territories, seems not to have been directly before the Convention which framed the original Constitution; and hence it is not recorded that the "thirty-nine," or any of them, while engaged on that instrument, expressed any opinion of that precise question.

In 1789, by the first Congress which sat under the Constitution, an act was passed to enforce the Ordinance of '87, including the prohibition of slavery in the Northwestern Territory. The bill for this act was reported by one of the "thirty-nine," Thomas Fitzsimmons, then a member of the House of Representatives from Pennsylvania. It went through all its stages without a word of opposition, and finally passed both branches without yeas and nays, which is equivalent to a unanimous passage. In this Congress were sixteen of the thirty-nine fathers who framed the original Constitution. They were John Langdon, Nicholas Gilman, Wm. S. Johnson, Roger Sherman, Robert Morris, Thos. Fitzsimmons, William Few, Abraham Baldwin, Rufus King, William Paterson, George Clymer, Richard Bassett, George Read, Pierce Butler, Daniel Carroll, James Madison.

This shows that, in their understanding, no line dividing local from federal authority, nor anything in the Constitution, properly forbade Congress to prohibit slavery in the federal territory; else both their fidelity to correct principle, and their oath to support the Constitution, would have constrained them to oppose the prohibition.

Again, George Washington, another of the "thirty-nine," was then President of the United States, and, as such, approved and signed the bill; thus completing its validity as a law, and thus showing that, in his understanding, no line dividing local from federal authority, nor anything in the Constitution, forbade the Federal Government, to control as to slavery in federal territory.

No great while after the adoption of the original Constitution, North Carolina ceded to the Federal Government the country now constituting the State of Tennessee; and a few years later Georgia ceded that which now constitutes the States of Mississippi and Alabama. In both deeds of cession it was made a condition by the ceding States that the Federal Government should not prohibit slavery in the ceded country. Besides this, slavery was then actually in the ceded country. Under these circumstances, Congress, on taking charge of these countries, did not absolutely prohibit slavery within them. But they did interfere with it—take control of it—even there, to a certain extent. In 1798, Congress organized the Territory of Mississippi. In the act of organization, they prohibited the bringing of slaves into the Territory, from any place without the United States, by fine, and giving freedom to slaves so brought. This act passed both branches of Congress without yeas and nays. In that Congress were three of the "thirty-nine" who framed the original Constitution. They were John Langdon, George Read and Abraham Baldwin. They all, probably, voted for it. Certainly they would have placed their opposition to it upon record, if, in their understanding, any line dividing local from federal authority, or anything in the Constitution, properly forbade the Federal Government to control as to slavery in federal territory.

In 1803, the Federal Government purchased the Louisiana country. Our former territorial acquisitions came from certain of our own States; but this Louisiana country was acquired from a foreign nation. In 1804, Congress gave a territorial organization to that part of it which now constitutes the State of Louisiana. New Orleans, lying within that part, was an old and comparatively large city. There were other considerable towns and settlements, and slavery was extensively and thoroughly intermingled with the people. Congress did not, in the Territorial Act, prohibit slavery; but they did interfere with it—take control of it—in a more marked and extensive way than they did in the case of Mississippi. The substance of the provision therein made, in relation to slaves, was:

<u>First</u>. That no slave should be imported into the territory from foreign parts.

<u>Second</u>. That no slave should be carried into it who had been imported into the United States since the first day of May, 1798.

<u>Third</u>. That no slave should be carried into it, except by the owner, and for his own use as a settler; the penalty in all the cases being a fine upon the violator of the law, and freedom to the slave.

This act also was passed without yeas and nays. In the Congress which passed it, there were two of the "thirty-nine." They were Abraham Baldwin and Jonathan Dayton. As stated in the case of Mississippi, it is probable they both voted for it. They would not have allowed it to pass without recording their opposition to it, if, in their understanding, it violated either the line properly dividing local from federal authority, or any provision of the Constitution.

In 1819-20, came and passed the Missouri question. Many votes were taken, by yeas and nays, in both branches of Congress, upon the various phases of the general question. Two of the "thirty-nine"—Rufus King and Charles Pinckney— were members of that Congress. Mr. King steadily voted for slavery prohibition and against all compromises, while Mr. Pinckney as steadily voted against slavery prohibition and against all compromises. By this, Mr. King showed that, in his understanding, no line dividing local from federal authority, nor anything in the Constitution, was violated by Congress prohibiting slavery in federal territory; while Mr. Pinckney, by his votes, showed that, in his understanding, there was some sufficient reason for opposing such prohibition in that case.

The cases I have mentioned are the only acts of the "thirty-nine," or of any of them, upon the direct issue, which I have been able to discover.

**PROOF:** To enumerate the persons who thus acted, as being four in 1784, two in 1787, seventeen in 1789, three in 1798, two in 1804, and two in 1819-20—there would be thirty of them. But this would be counting John Langdon, Roger Sherman, William Few, Rufus King, and George Read, each twice, and Abraham

Baldwin, three times. The true number of those of the "thirty-nine" whom I have shown to have acted upon the question, which, by the text, they understood better than we, is twenty-three, leaving sixteen not shown to have acted upon it in any way.

Here, then, we have twenty-three out of our thirty-nine fathers "who framed the Government under which we live," who have, upon their official responsibility and their corporal oaths, acted upon the very question which the text affirms they "understood just as well, and even better than we do now;" and twenty-one of them—a clear majority of the whole "thirty-nine"—so acting upon it as to make them guilty of gross political impropriety and willful perjury, if, in their understanding, any proper division between local and federal authority, or anything in the Constitution they had made themselves, and sworn to support, forbade the Federal Government to control as to slavery in the federal territories. Thus the twenty-one acted; and, as actions speak louder than words, so actions, under such responsibility, speak still louder.

Two of the twenty-three voted against Congressional prohibition of slavery in the federal territories, in the instances in which they acted upon the question. But for what reasons they so voted is not known. They may have done so because they thought a proper division of local from federal authority, or some provision or principle of the Constitution, stood in the way; or they may, without any such question, have voted against the prohibition, on what appeared to them to be sufficient grounds of expediency. No one who has sworn to support the Constitution, can conscientiously vote for what he understands to be an unconstitutional measure, however expedient he may think it; but one may and ought to vote against a measure which he deems constitutional, if, at the same time, he deems it inexpedient. It, therefore, would be unsafe to set down even the two who voted against the prohibition, as having done so because, in their understanding, any proper division of local from federal authority, or anything in the Constitution, forbade the Federal Government to control as to slavery in federal territory.

The remaining sixteen of the "thirty-nine," so far as I have discovered, have left no record of their understanding upon the direct question of federal control of slavery in the federal territories. But there is much reason to believe that their understanding upon that question would not have appeared different from that of their twenty-three compeers, had it been manifested at all.

For the purpose of adhering rigidly to the text, I have purposely omitted whatever understanding may have been manifested by any person, however distinguished, other than the thirty-nine fathers who framed the original Constitution; and, for the same reason, I have also omitted whatever understanding may have been manifested by any of the "thirty-nine" even, on any other phase of the general question of slavery. If we should look into their acts and declarations on those other phases, as the foreign slave trade, and the morality and policy of slavery generally, it would appear to us that on the direct question of federal control of slavery in federal territories, the sixteen, if they had acted at all, would probably have acted just as the twenty-three did. Among that sixteen were several of the most noted anti-slavery men of those times—as Dr. Franklin, Alexander Hamilton and Gouverneur Morris—while there was not one now known to have been otherwise, unless it may be John Rutledge, of South Carolina.

**CONCLUSION:** The sum of the whole is, that of our thirty-nine fathers who framed the original Constitution, twenty-one—a clear majority of the whole—certainly understood that no proper division of local from federal authority, nor any part of the Constitution, forbade the Federal Government to control slavery in the federal territories; while all the rest probably had the same understanding. Such, unquestionably, was the understanding of our fathers who framed the original Constitution; and the text affirms that they understood the question "better than we."[6]

## 16.4 ABRAHAM LINCOLN'S SECOND INAUGURAL ADDRESS

[Fellow Countrymen:]                                              March 4, 1865

**ENUNCIATION:** [Given] At this second appearing to take the oath of the presidential office, there is less occasion for an extended address than there was at the first. Then a statement, somewhat in detail, of a course to be pursued, seemed fitting and proper. Now, at the expiration of four years, during which public declarations have been constantly called forth on every point and phase of the great contest which still absorbs the attention, and engrosses the enerergies of the nation, little that is new could be presented. The progress of our arms, upon which all else chiefly depends, is as well known to the public as to myself; and it is, I trust, reasonably satisfactory and encouraging to all. [**Sought**] With high hope for the future, no prediction in regard to it is ventured.

**EXPOSITION:** On the occasion corresponding to this four years ago, all thoughts were anxiously directed to an impending civil-war. All dreaded it—all sought to avert it. While the inaugeral address was being delivered from this place, devoted altogether to <u>saving</u> the Union without war, insurgent agents were in the city seeking to <u>destroy</u> it without war—seeking to dissol[v]e the Union, and divide effects, by negotiation. Both parties deprecated war; but one of them would <u>make</u>

war rather than let the nation survive; and the other would <u>accept</u> war rather than let it perish. And the war came.

One eighth of the whole population were colored slaves, not distributed generally over the Union, but localized in the Southern part of it. These slaves constituted a peculiar and powerful interest. All knew that this interest was, somehow, the cause of the war.

To strengthen, perpetuate, and extend this interest was the object for which the insurgents would rend the Union, even by war; while the government claimed no right to do more than to restrict the territorial enlargement of it.

Neither party expected for the war, the magnitude, or the duration, which it has already attained. Neither anticipated that the <u>cause</u> of the conflict might cease with, or even before, the conflict itself should cease.

**SPECIFICATION:** Each looked for an easier triumph, and a result less fundamental and astounding.

**CONSTRUCTION:** Both read the same Bible, and pray to the same God; and each invokes His aid against the other. It may seem strange that any men should dare to ask a just God's assistance in wringing their bread from the sweat of other men's faces; but let us judge not that we be not judged.

**PROOF:** The prayers of both could not be answered; that of neither has been answered fully. The Almighty has His own purposes. "Woe unto the world because of offences! for it must needs be that offences come; but woe to that man by whom the offence cometh!" If we shall suppose that American Slavery is one of those offences which, in the providence of God, must needs come, but which, having continued through His appointed time, He now wills to remove, and that He gives to both North and South, this terrible war, as the woe due to those by whom the offence came, shall we discern therein any departure from those divine attributes which the believers in a Living God always ascribe to Him?

**CONCLUSION:** Fondly do we hope—fervently do we pray—that this mighty scourge of war may speedily pass away. Yet, if God wills that it continue, until all the wealth piled by the bond-man's two hundred and fifty years of unrequited toil shall be sunk, and until every drop of blood drawn with the lash, shall be paid by another drawn with the sword, as was said three thousand years ago, so still it must be said "the judgments of the Lord, are true and righteous altogether"

With malice toward none; with charity for all; with firmness in the right, as God gives us to see the right, let us strive on to finish the work we are in; to bind up the nation's wounds; to care for him who shall have borne the battle, and for his widow, and his orphan—to do all which may achieve and cherish a just, and a lasting peace, among ourselves, and with all nations.[7]

## QUESTIONS

ONE: How do the six elements of a proposition make the Declaration of Independence special?

TWO: How do the six elements of a proposition make the Virginia Statute for Religious Freedom special?

THREE: How do the six elements of a proposition make the first of the three propositions in Abraham Lincoln's Cooper Union Address special?

FOUR: How do the six elements of a proposition make Abraham Lincoln's Second Inaugural special?

FIVE: Who was the better writer, Thomas Jefferson or Abraham Lincoln?

SIX: What are the differences and similarities between Thomas Jefferson's six element style and Abraham Lincoln's six element style? What tends to be the difference in their subject matter? Who is more eloquent? Explain. Who is more persuasive? Explain.

# LESSON SEVENTEEN

# DEMARCATION EXERCISES

17.1 Silence - *February 11, 1788*

17.2 Perpetual Motion Machines - *December 27, 1812*

17.3 Barack Obama's Tucson Speech - *January 12, 2011*

17.4 Osama bin Laden is Dead - *May 1, 2011*

17.5 Michelle Obama, Democratic National Convention - *July 25, 2016*

Lesson 17 contains writings and speeches to demarcate into the elements of a proposition. Use hints in Lesson 18 to the extent needed. Lesson 19 contains suggested demarcations for Lesson 17 exercises. Hints plus suggested demarcations are not necessarily definitive. Most element borders should be clear in a composition that demarcates. Reasonable people can disagree where element lines should be drawn. Demarcating writings drafted within the structure of the six elements of a proposition facilitates understanding. It is a step toward elevating persuasive writing, and sharpening critical thinking.

**Enunciation:** "The **enunciation** states what is **given** and what is being **sought** from it." The **Enunciation** answers the question: *Why are we here?*

**Exposition:** "The **exposition** takes separately what is **given** and prepares it in advance for use in the investigation." The **Exposition** answers the question: *What additional facts are needed to know what to investigate?*

**Specification:** "The **specification** takes separately the thing that is **sought** and makes clear precisely what it is." The **Specification** answers the question: *What must be demonstrated to resolve what is sought?*

**Construction:** "The **construction** adds what is lacking in the **given** for finding what is **sought**." The **Construction** answers the question: *How do the facts lead to what is sought?*

**Proof:** "The **proof** draws the proposed inference by reasoning scientifically from the propositions that have been admitted." The **Proof** answers the question: *How does the admitted truth confirm the proposed inference?*

**Conclusion:** "The **conclusion** reverts to the **enunciation**, confirming what has been proved." The **Conclusion** answers the question: *What was demonstrated?*

## 17.1 SILENCE

In 1788, United States Minister to France Thomas Jefferson received a request from French lawyer, journalist, and revolutionary, Jean Pierre Brissot de Warville, to publicly oppose slavery.[1] Jefferson responded:

Sir                                                                    Paris Feb. 11. 1788.

I am very sensible of the honour you propose to me of becoming a member of the society for the abolition of the slave trade. You know that nobody wishes more ardently to see an abolition not only of the trade but of the condition of slavery: and certainly nobody will be more willing to encounter every sacrifice for that object. But the influence and information of the friends to this proposition in France will be far above the need of my association. I am here as a public servant; and those whom I serve having never yet been able to give their voice against this practice, it is decent for me to avoid too public a demonstration of my wishes to see it abolished. Without serving the cause here, it might render me less able to serve it beyond the water. I trust you will be sensible of the prudence of those motives therefore which govern my conduct on this occasion, and be assured of my wishes for the success of your undertaking and the sentiments of esteem and respect with which I have the honour to be Sir your most obedt. humble servt.,[2]

Th: Jefferson

## 17.2 PERPETUAL MOTION MACHINES

Robert Patterson was a mathematics professor at the University of Pennsylvania. He was a member of the American Philosophical Society. Patterson was one of five society members that President Jefferson asked to provide Meriwether Lewis with scientific instruction prior to the Lewis & Clark Expedition.[3]

Patterson's November 30, 1812, letter to Jefferson contained a description of Charles Redheffer's perpetual motion machine. Redhefffer charged men up to five dollars admission to see the machine. There was no admission charge for women. Redheffer claimed the machine generated enough power on its own to turn its gears.[4]

The actual power source was a hidden person turning a crank.[5]

In his November 30 letter, Patterson wrote:

> You have, Sir, I doubt not, seen, & perhaps heard a good deal of the machine called the perpetual motion, which has now for some time been exhibited near Germantown; and presuming that you will not be displeased to see a short description thereof, with the pretended rationale of its motion, I shall here make the attempt...[6]

Jefferson responded to Patterson's letter:[7]

> Dear Sir                                    Monticello Dec. 27. 12.
> After an absence of five weeks at a distant possession of mine to which I pay such visits three or four times a year, I find here your favor of Nov. 30. I am very thankful to you for the description of Redhefer's machine. I had never before been able to form an idea what his principle of deception was. he is the first of the inventors of perpetual motion, within my knolege, who has had the cunning to put his visitors on a false pursuit, by amusing them with a sham machinery, whose loose & vibratory motion might impose on them the belief that it is the real source of the motion they see. to this device he is indebted for a more extensive delusion than I have before witnessed on this point. we are full of it as far as this state, & I know not how much farther. in Richmond they have done me the honor to quote me as having said that it was a possible thing. a poor Frenchman who called on me the other day with another invention of perpetual motion, assured me that Dr Franklin, many years ago expressed his opinion to him that it was not impossible. without

entering into contest on this abuse of the Doctor's name, I gave him the answer I had given to others before, that the almighty himself could not construct a machine of perpetual motion, while the laws exist which he has prescribed for the government of matter in our system: that the equilibrium established by him between cause & effect must be suspended to effect that purpose. but Redhefer seems to be reaping a rich harvest from the public deception. the office of Science is to instruct the ignorant. would it be unworthy of some one of it's votaries who witness this deception to give a popular demonstration of the insufficiency of the ostensible machinery, & of course of the necessary existence of some hidden mover? and who could do it with more effect on the public mind than yourself?...

Th: Jefferson

## 17.3 Barack Obama's Tucson Speech

On January 8, 2011, Member of Congress Gabrielle Giffords held a "Congress on Your Corner" event in Tucson, Arizona. At the event, a shooter killed six people and injured 13 people. Giffords was among the injured.[8] On January 12, 2011, President Barack Obama spoke at the University of Arizona in Tucson:[9]

THE PRESIDENT: Thank you. (Applause.) Thank you very much. Please, please be seated. (Applause.)

To the families of those we've lost; to all who called them friends; to the students of this university, the public servants who are gathered here, the people of Tucson and the people of Arizona: I have come here tonight as an American who, like all Americans, kneels to pray with you today and will stand by you tomorrow. (Applause.)

There is nothing I can say that will fill the sudden hole torn in your hearts. But know this: The hopes of a nation are here tonight. We mourn with you for the fallen. We join you in your grief. And we add our faith to yours that Representative Gabrielle Giffords and the other living victims of this tragedy will pull through. (Applause.)

Scripture tells us:

There is a river whose streams make glad the city of God,
the holy place where the Most High dwells.
God is within her, she will not fall;
God will help her at break of day.

On Saturday morning, Gabby, her staff and many of her constituents gathered outside a supermarket to exercise their right to peaceful assembly and free speech. (Applause.) They were fulfilling a central tenet of the democracy envisioned by our founders — representatives of the people answering questions to their constituents, so as to carry their concerns back to our nation's capital. Gabby called it "Congress on Your Corner" — just an updated version of government of and by and for the people. (Applause.)

And that quintessentially American scene, that was the scene that was shattered by a gunman's bullets. And the six people who lost their lives on Saturday — they, too, represented what is best in us, what is best in America. (Applause.)

Judge John Roll served our legal system for nearly 40 years. (Applause.) A graduate of this university and a graduate of this law school — (applause) — Judge Roll was recommended for the federal bench by John McCain 20 years ago — (applause) — appointed by President George H.W. Bush and rose to become Arizona's chief federal judge. (Applause.)

His colleagues described him as the hardest-working judge within the Ninth Circuit. He was on his way back from attending Mass, as he did every day, when he decided to stop by and say hi to his representative. John is survived by his loving wife, Maureen, his three sons and his five beautiful grandchildren. (Applause.)

George and Dorothy Morris — "Dot" to her friends — were high school sweethearts who got married and had two daughters. They did everything together — traveling the open road in their RV, enjoying what their friends called a 50-year honeymoon. Saturday morning, they went by the Safeway to hear what their congresswoman had to say. When gunfire rang out, George, a former Marine, instinctively tried to shield his wife. (Applause.) Both were shot. Dot passed away.

A New Jersey native, Phyllis Schneck retired to Tucson to beat the snow. But in the summer, she would return East, where her world revolved around her three children, her seven grandchildren and 2-year-old great-granddaughter. A gifted quilter, she'd often work under a favorite tree, or sometimes she'd sew aprons with the logos of the Jets and the Giants — (laughter) — to give out at the church where she volunteered. A Republican, she took a liking to Gabby, and wanted to get to know her better. (Applause.)

Dorwan and Mavy Stoddard grew up in Tucson together — about 70 years ago. They moved apart and started their own respective families. But after both were widowed they found their way back here, to, as one of Mavy's daughters put it, "be boyfriend and girlfriend again." (Laughter.)

When they weren't out on the road in their motor home, you could find them just up the road, helping folks in need at the Mountain Avenue Church of Christ. A retired construction worker, Dorwan spent his spare time fixing up the church along with his dog, Tux. His final act of selflessness was to dive on top of his wife, sacrificing his life for hers. (Applause.)

Everything — everything — Gabe Zimmerman did, he did with passion. (Applause.) But his true passion was helping people. As Gabby's outreach director, he made the cares of thousands of her constituents his own, seeing to it that seniors got the Medicare benefits that they had earned, that veterans got the medals and the care that they deserved, that government was working for ordinary folks. He died doing what he loved — talking with people and seeing how he could help. And Gabe is survived by his parents, Ross and Emily, his brother, Ben, and his fiancée, Kelly, who he planned to marry next year. (Applause.)

And then there is nine-year-old Christina Taylor Green. Christina was an A student; she was a dancer; she was a gymnast; she was a swimmer. She decided that she wanted to be the first woman to play in the Major Leagues, and as the only girl on her Little League team, no one put it past her. (Applause.)

She showed an appreciation for life uncommon for a girl her age. She'd remind her mother, "We are so blessed. We have the best life." And she'd pay those blessings back by participating in a charity that helped children who were less fortunate.

Our hearts are broken by their sudden passing. Our hearts are broken — and yet, our hearts also have reason for fullness.

Our hearts are full of hope and thanks for the 13 Americans who survived the shooting, including the congresswoman many of them went to see on Saturday.

I have just come from the University Medical Center, just a mile from here, where our friend Gabby courageously fights to recover even as we speak. And I want to tell you — her husband Mark is here and he allows me to share this with you — right after we went to visit, a few minutes after we left her room and some of her colleagues in Congress were in the room, Gabby opened her eyes for the first time. (Applause.) Gabby opened her eyes for the first time. (Applause.)

Gabby opened her eyes. Gabby opened her eyes, so I can tell you she knows we are here. She knows we love her. And she knows that we are rooting for her through what is undoubtedly going to be a difficult journey. We are there for her. (Applause.)

Our hearts are full of thanks for that good news, and our hearts are full of gratitude for those who saved others. We are grateful to Daniel Hernandez — (applause) — a volunteer in Gabby's office. (Applause.)

And, Daniel, I'm sorry, you may deny it, but we've decided you are a hero because — (applause) — you ran through the chaos to minister to your boss, and tended to her wounds and helped keep her alive. (Applause.)

We are grateful to the men who tackled the gunman as he stopped to reload. (Applause.) Right over there. (Applause.) We are grateful for petite Patricia Maisch, who wrestled away the killer's ammunition, and undoubtedly saved some lives. (Applause.) And we are grateful for the doctors and nurses and first responders who worked wonders to heal those who'd been hurt. We are grateful to them. (Applause.)

These men and women remind us that heroism is found not only on the fields of battle. They remind us that heroism does not require special training or physical strength. Heroism is here, in the hearts of so many of our fellow citizens, all around us, just waiting to be summoned — as it was on Saturday morning. Their actions, their selflessness poses a challenge to each of us. It raises a question of what, beyond prayers and expressions of concern, is required of us going forward. How can we honor the fallen? How can we be true to their memory?

You see, when a tragedy like this strikes, it is part of our nature to demand explanations — to try and pose some order on the chaos and make sense out of that which seems senseless. Already we've seen a national conversation commence, not only about the motivations behind these killings, but about everything from the merits of gun safety laws to the adequacy of our mental health system. And much of this process, of debating what might be done to prevent such tragedies in the future, is an essential ingredient in our exercise of self-government.

But at a time when our discourse has become so sharply polarized — at a time when we are far too eager to lay the blame for all that ails the world at the feet of those who happen to think differently than we do — it's important for us to pause for a moment and make sure that we're talking with each other in a way that heals, not in a way that wounds. (Applause.)

Scripture tells us that there is evil in the world, and that terrible things happen for reasons that defy human understanding. In the words of Job, "When I looked for light, then came darkness." Bad things happen, and we have to guard against simple explanations in the aftermath.

For the truth is none of us can know exactly what triggered this vicious attack. None of us can know with any certainty what might have stopped these shots from being fired, or what thoughts lurked in the inner recesses of a violent man's mind. Yes, we have to examine all the facts behind this tragedy. We cannot and will not be passive in the face of such violence. We should be willing to challenge old assumptions in order to lessen the prospects of such violence in the future. (Applause.) But what we cannot do is use this tragedy as one more occasion to turn on each other. (Applause.) That we cannot do. (Applause.) That we cannot do.

As we discuss these issues, let each of us do so with a good dose of humility. Rather than pointing fingers or assigning blame, let's use this occasion to expand our moral imaginations, to listen to each other more carefully, to sharpen our instincts for empathy and remind ourselves of all the ways that our hopes and dreams are bound together. (Applause.)

After all, that's what most of us do when we lose somebody in our family — especially if the loss is unexpected. We're shaken out of our routines. We're forced to look inward. We reflect on the past: Did we spend enough time with an aging parent, we wonder. Did we express our gratitude for all the sacrifices that they made for us? Did we tell a spouse just how desperately we loved them, not just once in a while but every single day?

So sudden loss causes us to look backward — but it also forces us to look forward; to reflect on the present and the future, on the manner in which we live our lives and nurture our relationships with those who are still with us. (Applause.)

We may ask ourselves if we've shown enough kindness and generosity and compassion to the people in our lives. Perhaps we question whether we're doing right by our children, or our community, whether our priorities are in order.

We recognize our own mortality, and we are reminded that in the fleeting time we have on this Earth, what matters is not wealth, or status, or power, or fame — but rather, how well we have loved — (applause)— and what small part we have played in making the lives of other people better. (Applause.)

And that process — that process of reflection, of making sure we align our values with our actions — that, I believe, is what a tragedy like this requires.

For those who were harmed, those who were killed — they are part of our family, an American family 300 million strong. (Applause.) We may not have known them personally, but surely we see ourselves in them. In George and Dot, in Dorwan and Mavy, we sense the abiding love we have for our own husbands, our own wives, our own life partners. Phyllis — she's our mom or our grandma; Gabe our brother or son. (Applause.) In Judge Roll, we recognize not only a man who prized his family and doing his job well, but also a man who embodied America's fidelity to the law. (Applause.)

And in Gabby — in Gabby, we see a reflection of our public-spiritedness; that desire to participate in that sometimes frustrating, sometimes contentious, but always necessary and never-ending process to form a more perfect union. (Applause.)

And in Christina — in Christina we see all of our children. So curious, so trusting, so energetic, so full of magic. So deserving of our love. And so deserving of our good example.

If this tragedy prompts reflection and debate — as it should — let's make sure it's worthy of those we have lost. (Applause.) Let's make sure it's not on the usual plane of politics and point-scoring and pettiness that drifts away in the next news cycle.

The loss of these wonderful people should make every one of us strive to be better. To be better in our private lives, to be better friends and neighbors and coworkers and parents. And if, as has been discussed in recent days, their death helps usher in more civility in our public discourse, let us remember it is not because a simple lack of civility caused this tragedy — it did not — but rather because only a more civil and honest public discourse can help us face up to the challenges of our nation in a way that would make them proud. (Applause.)

We should be civil because we want to live up to the example of public servants like John Roll and Gabby Giffords, who knew first and foremost that we are all Americans, and that we can question each other's ideas without questioning each other's love of country and that our task, working together, is to constantly widen the circle of our concern so that we bequeath the American Dream to future generations. (Applause.)

They believed — they believed, and I believe that we can be better. Those who died here, those who saved life here — they help me believe. We may not be able to stop all evil in the world, but I know that how we treat one another, that's entirely up to us. (Applause.)

And I believe that for all our imperfections, we are full of decency and goodness, and that the forces that divide us are not as strong as those that unite us. (Applause.)

That's what I believe, in part because that's what a child like Christina Taylor Green believed. (Applause.)

Imagine — imagine for a moment, here was a young girl who was just becoming aware of our democracy; just beginning to understand the obligations of citizenship; just starting to glimpse the fact that some day she, too, might play a part in shaping her nation's future. She had been elected to her student council. She saw public service as something exciting and hopeful. She was off to meet her congresswoman, someone she was sure was good and important and might be a role model. She saw all this through the eyes of a child, undimmed by the cynicism or vitriol that we adults all too often just take for granted.

I want to live up to her expectations. (Applause.) I want our democracy to be as good as Christina imagined it. I want America to be as good as she imagined it. (Applause.) All of us — we should do everything we can to make sure this country lives up to our children's expectations. (Applause.)

As has already been mentioned, Christina was given to us on September 11th, 2001, one of 50 babies born that day to be pictured in a book called "Faces of Hope." On either side of her photo in that book were simple wishes for a child's life. "I hope you help those in need," read one. "I hope you know all the words to the National Anthem and sing it with your hand over your heart." (Applause.) "I hope you jump in rain puddles."

If there are rain puddles in Heaven, Christina is jumping in them today. (Applause.) And here on this Earth — here on this Earth, we place our hands over our hearts, and we commit ourselves as Americans to forging a country that is forever worthy of her gentle, happy spirit.

May God bless and keep those we've lost in restful and eternal peace. May He love and watch over the survivors. And may He bless the United States of America. (Applause.)

### 17.4 Osama bin Laden is Dead

May 1, 2011[10]

THE PRESIDENT: Good evening. Tonight, I can report to the American people and to the world that the United States has conducted an operation that killed Osama bin Laden, the leader of al Qaeda, and a terrorist who's responsible for the murder of thousands of innocent men, women, and children.

It was nearly 10 years ago that a bright September day was darkened by the worst attack on the American people in our history. The images of 9/11 are seared into our national memory — hijacked planes cutting through a cloudless September sky; the Twin Towers collapsing to the ground; black smoke billowing up from the Pentagon; the wreckage of Flight 93 in Shanksville, Pennsylvania, where the actions of heroic citizens saved even more heartbreak and destruction.

And yet we know that the worst images are those that were unseen to the world. The empty seat at the dinner table. Children who were forced to grow up without their mother or their father. Parents who would never know the feeling of their child's embrace. Nearly 3,000 citizens taken from us, leaving a gaping hole in our hearts.

On September 11, 2001, in our time of grief, the American people came together. We offered our neighbors a hand, and we offered the wounded our blood. We reaffirmed our ties to each other, and our love of community and country. On that day, no matter where we came from, what God we prayed to, or what race or ethnicity we were, we were united as one American family.

We were also united in our resolve to protect our nation and to bring those who committed this vicious attack to justice. We quickly learned that the 9/11 attacks were carried out by al Qaeda — an organization headed by Osama bin Laden, which had openly declared war on the United States and was committed to killing innocents in our country and around the globe. And so we went to war against al Qaeda to protect our citizens, our friends, and our allies.

Over the last 10 years, thanks to the tireless and heroic work of our military and our counterterrorism professionals, we've made great strides in that effort. We've disrupted terrorist attacks and strengthened our homeland defense. In Afghanistan, we removed the Taliban government, which had given bin Laden and al Qaeda safe haven and support. And around the globe, we worked with our friends and allies to capture or kill scores of al Qaeda terrorists, including several who were a part of the 9/11 plot.

Yet Osama bin Laden avoided capture and escaped across the Afghan border into Pakistan. Meanwhile, al Qaeda continued to operate from along that border and operate through its affiliates across the world.

And so shortly after taking office, I directed Leon Panetta, the director of the CIA, to make the killing or capture of bin Laden the top priority of our war against al Qaeda, even as we continued our broader efforts to disrupt, dismantle, and defeat his network.

Then, last August, after years of painstaking work by our intelligence community, I was briefed on a possible lead to bin Laden. It was far from certain, and it took many months to run this thread to ground. I met repeatedly with my national security team as we developed more information about the possibility that we had located bin Laden hiding within a compound deep inside of Pakistan. And finally, last week, I determined that we had enough intelligence to take action, and authorized an operation to get Osama bin Laden and bring him to justice.

Today, at my direction, the United States launched a targeted operation against that compound in Abbottabad, Pakistan. A small team of Americans carried out the operation with extraordinary courage and capability. No Americans were harmed. They took care to avoid civilian casualties. After a firefight, they killed Osama bin Laden and took custody of his body.

For over two decades, bin Laden has been al Qaeda's leader and symbol, and has continued to plot attacks against our country and our friends and allies. The death of bin Laden marks the most significant achievement to date in our nation's effort to defeat al Qaeda.

Yet his death does not mark the end of our effort. There's no doubt that al Qaeda will continue to pursue attacks against us. We must — and we will — remain vigilant at home and abroad.

As we do, we must also reaffirm that the United States is not — and never will be — at war with Islam. I've made clear, just as President Bush did shortly after 9/11, that our war is not against Islam. Bin Laden was not a Muslim leader; he was a mass murderer of Muslims. Indeed, al Qaeda has slaughtered scores of Muslims in many countries, including our own. So his demise should be welcomed by all who believe in peace and human dignity.

Over the years, I've repeatedly made clear that we would take action within Pakistan if we knew where bin Laden was. That is what we've done. But it's important to note that our counterterrorism cooperation with Pakistan helped lead us to bin Laden and the compound where he was hiding. Indeed, bin Laden had declared war against Pakistan as well, and ordered attacks against the Pakistani people.

Tonight, I called President Zardari, and my team has also spoken with their Pakistani counterparts. They agree that this is a good and historic day for both of our nations. And going forward, it is essential that Pakistan continue to join us in the fight against al Qaeda and its affiliates.

The American people did not choose this fight. It came to our shores, and started with the senseless slaughter of our citizens. After nearly 10 years of service, struggle, and sacrifice, we know well the costs of war. These efforts weigh on me every time I, as Commander-in-Chief, have to sign a letter to a family that has lost a loved one, or look into the eyes of a service member who's been gravely wounded.

So Americans understand the costs of war. Yet as a country, we will never tolerate our security being threatened, nor stand idly by when our people have been killed. We will be relentless in defense of our citizens and our friends and allies. We will be true to the values that make us who we are. And on nights like this one, we can say to those families who have lost loved ones to al Qaeda's terror: Justice has been done.

Tonight, we give thanks to the countless intelligence and counterterrorism professionals who've worked tirelessly to achieve this outcome. The American people do not see their work, nor know their names. But tonight, they feel the satisfaction of their work and the result of their pursuit of justice.

We give thanks for the men who carried out this operation, for they exemplify the professionalism, patriotism, and unparalleled courage of those who serve our country. And they are part of a generation that has borne the heaviest share of the burden since that September day.

Finally, let me say to the families who lost loved ones on 9/11 that we have never forgotten your loss, nor wavered in our commitment to see that we do whatever it takes to prevent another attack on our shores.

And tonight, let us think back to the sense of unity that prevailed on 9/11. I know that it has, at times, frayed. Yet today's achievement is a testament to the greatness of our country and the determination of the American people.

The cause of securing our country is not complete. But tonight, we are once again reminded that America can do whatever we set our mind to. That is the story of our history, whether it's the pursuit of prosperity for our people, or the struggle for equality for all our citizens; our commitment to stand up for our values abroad, and our sacrifices to make the world a safer place.

Let us remember that we can do these things not just because of wealth or power, but because of who we are: one nation, under God, indivisible, with liberty and justice for all.

Thank you. May God bless you. And may God bless the United States of America.

## 17.5 Michelle Obama, Democratic National Convention

Philadelphia, Pennsylvania, July 25, 2016[11]

Thank you all. (Applause.) Thank you so much. You know, it's hard to believe that it has been eight years since I first came to this convention to talk with you about why I thought my husband should be President. (Applause.) Remember how I told you about his character and conviction, his decency and his grace — the traits that we've seen every day that he's served our country in the White House.

I also told you about our daughters — how they are the heart of our hearts, the center of our world. And during our time in the White House, we've had the joy of watching them grow from bubbly little girls into poised young women — a journey that started soon after we arrived in Washington, when they set off for their first day at their new school.

I will never forget that winter morning as I watched our girls, just seven and ten years old, pile into those black SUVs with all those big men with guns. (Laughter.) And I saw their little faces pressed up against the window, and the only thing I could think was, "What have we done?" (Laughter.) See, because at that moment, I realized that our time in the White House would form the foundation for who they would become, and how well we managed this experience could truly make or break them.

That is what Barack and I think about every day as we try to guide and protect our girls through the challenges of this unusual life in the spotlight — how we urge them to ignore those who question their father's citizenship or faith. (Applause.) How we insist that the hateful language they hear from public figures on TV does not represent the true spirit of this country. (Applause.) How we explain that when someone is cruel, or acts like a bully, you don't stoop to their level — no, our motto is, when they go low, we go high. (Applause.)

With every word we utter, with every action we take, we know our kids are watching us. We as parents are their most important role models. And let me tell you, Barack and I take that same approach to our jobs as President and First Lady, because we know that our words and actions matter not just to our girls, but to children across this country — kids who tell us, "I saw you on TV, I wrote a report on you for school." Kids like the little black boy who looked up at my husband, his eyes wide with hope, and he wondered, "Is my hair like yours?" (Applause.)

And make no mistake about it, this November, when we go to the polls, that is what we're deciding — not Democrat or Republican, not left or right. No, this election, and every election, is about who will have the power to shape our children for the next four or eight years of their lives. (Applause.)  And I am here tonight because in this election, there is only one person who I trust with that responsibility, only one person who I believe is truly qualified to be President of the United States, and that is our friend, Hillary Clinton. (Applause.)

See, I trust Hillary to lead this country because I've seen her lifelong devotion to our nation's children — not just her own daughter, who she has raised to perfection — (applause) — but every child who needs a champion: Kids who take the long way to school to avoid the gangs. Kids who wonder how they'll ever afford college. Kids whose parents don't speak a word of English but dream of a better life. Kids who look to us to determine who and what they can be.

You see, Hillary has spent decades doing the relentless, thankless work to actually make a difference in their lives — (applause) -- advocating for kids with disabilities as a young lawyer. Fighting for children's health care as First Lady and for quality child care in the Senate. And when she didn't win the nomination eight years ago, she didn't get angry or disillusioned. (Applause.) Hillary did not pack up and go home. Because as a true public servant, Hillary knows that this is so much bigger than her own desires and disappointments. (Applause.) So she proudly stepped up to serve our country once again as Secretary of State, traveling the globe to keep our kids safe.

And look, there were plenty of moments when Hillary could have decided that this work was too hard, that the price of public service was too high, that she was tired of being picked apart for how she looks or how she talks or even how she laughs. But here's the thing — what I admire most about Hillary is that she never buckles under pressure. (Applause.) She never takes the easy way out. And Hillary Clinton has never quit on anything in her life. (Applause.)

And when I think about the kind of President that I want for my girls and all our children, that's what I want. I want someone with the proven strength to persevere. Someone who knows this job and takes it seriously. Someone who understands that the issues a President faces are not black and white and cannot be boiled down to 140 characters. (Applause.) Because when you have the nuclear codes at your fingertips and the military in your command, you can't make snap decisions. You can't have a thin skin or a tendency to lash out. You need to be steady, and measured, and well-informed. (Applause.)

I want a President with a record of public service, someone whose life's work shows our children that we don't chase fame and fortune for ourselves, we fight to give everyone a chance to succeed — (applause) — and we give back, even when we're struggling ourselves, because we know that there is always someone worse off, and there but for the grace of God go I. (Applause.)

I want a President who will teach our children that everyone in this country matters — a President who truly believes in the vision that our founders put forth all those years ago: That we are all created equal, each a beloved part of the great American story. (Applause.) And when crisis hits, we don't turn against each other — no, we listen to each other. We lean on each other. Because we are always stronger together. (Applause.)

And I am here tonight because I know that that is the kind of president that Hillary Clinton will be. And that's why, in this election, I'm with her. (Applause.)

You see, Hillary understands that the President is about one thing and one thing only — it's about leaving something better for our kids. That's how we've always moved this country forward — by all of us coming together on behalf of our children — folks who volunteer to coach that team, to teach that Sunday school class because they know it takes a village. Heroes of every color and creed who wear the uniform and risk their lives to keep passing down those blessings of liberty.

Police officers and protestors in Dallas who all desperately want to keep our children safe. (Applause.) People who lined up in Orlando to donate blood because it could have been their son, their daughter in that club. (Applause.) Leaders like Tim Kaine — (applause) — who show our kids what decency and devotion look like. Leaders like Hillary Clinton, who has the guts and the grace to keep coming back and putting those cracks in that highest and hardest glass ceiling until she finally breaks through, lifting all of us along with her. (Applause.)

That is the story of this country, the story that has brought me to this stage tonight, the story of generations of people who felt the lash of bondage, the shame of servitude, the sting of segregation, but who kept on striving and hoping and doing what needed to be done so that today, I wake up every morning in a house that was built by slaves — (applause) — and I watch my daughters — two beautiful, intelligent, black young women — playing with their dogs on the White House lawn. (Applause.) And because of Hillary Clinton, my daughters — and all our sons and daughters — now take for granted that a woman can be President of the United States. (Applause.)

So don't let anyone ever tell you that this country isn't great, that somehow we need to make it great again. Because this, right now, is the greatest country on earth. (Applause.) And as my daughters prepare to set out into the world, I want a leader who is worthy of that truth, a leader who is worthy of my girls' promise and all our kids' promise, a leader who will be guided every day by the love and hope and impossibly big dreams that we all have for our children.

So in this election, we cannot sit back and hope that everything works out for the best. We cannot afford to be tired, or frustrated, or cynical. No, hear me — between now and November, we need to do what we did eight years ago and four years ago: We need to knock on every door. We need to get out every vote. We need to pour every last ounce of our passion and our strength and our love for this country into electing Hillary Clinton as President of the United States of America.

Let's get to work. Thank you all, and God bless.

## QUESTIONS

ONE: Which writing in this lesson was the easiest to demarcate? Why?

TWO: Which writing in this lesson was the most difficult to demarcate? Why?

THREE: Which writing in this lesson had the greatest impact? Why? How?

FOUR: Which writing in this lesson did you like the most? Why?

# LESSON EIGHTEEN

# HINTS FOR DEMARCATION EXERCISES

## 18.1 SILENCE - DEMARCATION HINTS

The **Enunciation's given** acknowledges the honor given to Jefferson. The **sought** portrays Jefferson as an abolitionist.

The **Exposition** expresses Jefferson's willingness to sacrifice for the cause as a basis for the demonstration's Investigation.

The **Specification** states the lack of need in France for Jefferson's influence.

The **Construction** factually presented Jefferson's impotence on this subject domestically.

The **Proof** argues nothing good can come from Jefferson going public on the issue.

The **Conclusion** apologetically restates what was demonstrated.

## 18.2 PERPETUAL MOTION - DEMARCATION HINTS

This demarcation is challenging.

The **Enunciation's given** briefly sets up the "existence" of a perpetual motion machine. The **sought** is to figure out the deception of the machine.

The **Exposition** expresses the sham, but struggles to inform a strategy to find facts that explain the deception.

The **Specification** frames a deception.

The **Construction** alludes to misquotation of Jefferson and Franklin.

The Proof can be viewed as a Jefferson rant.

The **Conclusion** suggests the addressee, Robert Patterson, would be the most credible to expose the deception.

## 18.3 BARACK OBAMA'S TUCSON SPEECH DEMARCATION HINTS

This is one of President Obama's first speeches to demarcate. The **Enunciation** is short. The **given** identifies those who are the object of the speech. The **sought** identifies a plain, straightforward goal: pray today; stand by tomorrow.

The **Exposition** describes the impossibility of the President's task. It also contains personal facts about the victims.

The **Specification** asks how we can honor the fallen.

The **Construction** discusses the nature of tragedy.

The Proof speaks of humility, sudden loss, and the importance of aligning our actions with our values. "We are full of decency and goodness."

The **Conclusion**: "May God bless and keep those we've lost in restful and eternal peace. May He love and watch over the survivors."

Some commentators at the time compared this speech to Lincoln's Gettysburg Address.[1] They likely did not realize how structurally correct they were.

## 18.4 OSAMA BIN LADEN IS DEAD - DEMARCATION HINTS

The **Enunciation's given** is a recitation of events. The **sought** speaks of going to war.

The **Exposition** speaks of many successes and one major failure.

The **Specification** identifies the Commander in Chief's top priority.

The **Construction** recites the death of bin Laden and related facts.

The Proof focuses on the nature of this war.

The **Conclusion** recites, "The cause of securing our country is not complete." The President then talks about American history and character.

## 18.5 MICHELLE OBAMA, DEMOCRATIC NATIONAL CONVENTION - DEMARCATION HINTS

The **Enunciation's given** reference's Michelle Obama's family. Every element refers to children. The **sought** connects White House performance with the foundation for what the Obama daughters will become.

The **Exposition** expresses the importance of setting examples. Here it focuses on, "...our kids are watching us."

The **Specification** asks who will have presidential power to shape the nation's children.

The **Construction** arrays facts regarding who should have the power to shape the nation's children.

The **Proof** argues which candidate would be better for children.

The **Conclusion** recites which candidate Michelle Obama feels is more worthy of the dreams parents have for their children.

# Lesson Nineteen

## Suggested Demarcations

### 19.1 Silence

To Brissot de Warville

Sir                                                      Paris Feb. 11. 1788.

**Enunciation:** [**Given**] I am very sensible of the honour you propose to me of becoming a member of the society for the abolition of the slave trade. [**Sought**] You know that nobody wishes more ardently to see an abolition not only of the trade but of the condition of slavery:

**Exposition:** and certainly nobody will be more willing to encounter every sacrifice for that object.

**Specification:** But the influence and information of the friends to this proposition in France will be far above the need of my association.

**Construction:** I am here as a public servant; and those whom I serve having never yet been able to give their voice against this practice,

**Proof:** it is decent for me to avoid too public a demonstration of my wishes to see it abolished. Without serving the cause here, it might render me less able to serve it beyond the water.

**Conclusion:** I trust you will be sensible of the prudence of those motives therefore which govern my conduct on this occasion, and be assured of my wishes for the success of your undertaking and the sentiments of esteem and respect with which I have the honour to be Sir your most obedt. humble servt.,

Th: Jefferson

## 19.2 PERPETUAL MOTION MACHINES

Dear Sir                                      Monticello Dec. 27. 12.

**Enunciation:** [**Given**] After an absence of five weeks at a distant possession of mine to which I pay such visits three or four times a year, I find here your favor of Nov. 30. I am very thankful to you for the description of Redhefer's machine. [**Sought**] I had never before been able to form an idea of what his principle of deception was.

**Exposition:** he is the first of the inventors of perpetual motion, within my knolege, who has had the cunning to put his visitors on a false pursuit, by amusing them with a sham machinery, whose loose & vibratory motion might impose on them the belief that it is the real source of the motion they see.

**Specification:** to this device he is indebted for a more extensive delusion than I have before witnessed on this point.

**Construction:** we are full of it as far as this state, & I know not how much farther. in Richmond they have done me the honor to quote me as having said that it was a possible thing. a poor Frenchman who called on me the other day with another invention of perpetual motion, assured me that Dr Franklin, many years ago expressed his opinion to him that it was not impossible.

**Proof:** without entering into contest on this abuse of the Doctor's name, I gave him the answer I had given to others before, that the almighty himself could not construct a machine of perpetual motion, while the laws exist which he has prescribed for the government of matter in our system: that the equilibrium established by him between cause & effect must be suspended to effect that purpose. but Redhefer seems to be reaping a rich harvest from the public deception. the office of Science is to instruct the ignorant. would it be unworthy of some one of it's votaries who witness this deception to give a popular demonstration of the insufficiency of the ostensible machinery, & of course of the necessary existence of some hidden mover?

**Conclusion:** and who could do it with more effect on the public mind than yourself?

Th: Jefferson

## 19.3 Barack Obama's Tucson Speech

McKale Memorial Center, University of Arizona
Tucson, Arizona, January 12, 2011

THE PRESIDENT: Thank you. (Applause.) Thank you very much. Please, please be seated. (Applause.)

**Enunciation:** [**Given**] To the families of those we've lost; to all who called them friends; to the students of this university, the public servants who are gathered here, the people of Tucson and the people of Arizona: [**Sought**] I have come here tonight as an American who, like all Americans, kneels to pray with you today and will stand by you tomorrow. (Applause.)

**Exposition:** There is nothing I can say that will fill the sudden hole torn in your hearts. But know this: The hopes of a nation are here tonight. We mourn with you for the fallen. We join you in your grief. And we add our faith to yours that Representative Gabrielle Giffords and the other living victims of this tragedy will pull through. (Applause.)

Scripture tells us:

There is a river whose streams make glad the city of God,
the holy place where the Most High dwells.
God is within her, she will not fall;
God will help her at break of day.

On Saturday morning, Gabby, her staff and many of her constituents gathered outside a supermarket to exercise their right to peaceful assembly and free speech. (Applause.) They were fulfilling a central tenet of the democracy envisioned by our founders — representatives of the people answering questions to their constituents, so as to carry their concerns back to our nation's capital. Gabby called it "Congress on Your Corner" — just an updated version of government of and by and for the people. (Applause.)

And that quintessentially American scene, that was the scene that was shattered by a gunman's bullets. And the six people who lost their lives on Saturday — they, too, represented what is best in us, what is best in America. (Applause.)

Judge John Roll served our legal system for nearly 40 years. (Applause.) A graduate of this university and a graduate of this law school — (applause) — Judge Roll was recommended for the federal bench by John McCain 20 years ago —

(applause) — appointed by President George H.W. Bush and rose to become Arizona's chief federal judge. (Applause.)

His colleagues described him as the hardest-working judge within the Ninth Circuit. He was on his way back from attending Mass, as he did every day, when he decided to stop by and say hi to his representative. John is survived by his loving wife, Maureen, his three sons and his five beautiful grandchildren. (Applause.)

George and Dorothy Morris — "Dot" to her friends — were high school sweethearts who got married and had two daughters. They did everything together — traveling the open road in their RV, enjoying what their friends called a 50-year honeymoon. Saturday morning, they went by the Safeway to hear what their congresswoman had to say. When gunfire rang out, George, a former Marine, instinctively tried to shield his wife. (Applause.) Both were shot. Dot passed away.

A New Jersey native, Phyllis Schneck retired to Tucson to beat the snow. But in the summer, she would return East, where her world revolved around her three children, her seven grandchildren and 2-year-old great-granddaughter. A gifted quilter, she'd often work under a favorite tree, or sometimes she'd sew aprons with the logos of the Jets and the Giants — (laughter) — to give out at the church where she volunteered. A Republican, she took a liking to Gabby, and wanted to get to know her better. (Applause.)

Dorwan and Mavy Stoddard grew up in Tucson together — about 70 years ago. They moved apart and started their own respective families. But after both were widowed they found their way back here, to, as one of Mavy's daughters put it, "be boyfriend and girlfriend again." (Laughter.)

When they weren't out on the road in their motor home, you could find them just up the road, helping folks in need at the Mountain Avenue Church of Christ. A retired construction worker, Dorwan spent his spare time fixing up the church along with his dog, Tux. His final act of selflessness was to dive on top of his wife, sacrificing his life for hers. (Applause.)

Everything — everything — Gabe Zimmerman did, he did with passion. (Applause.) But his true passion was helping people. As Gabby's outreach director, he made the cares of thousands of her constituents his own, seeing to it that seniors got the Medicare benefits that they had earned, that veterans got the medals and the care that they deserved, that government was working for ordinary folks. He died doing what he loved — talking with people and seeing how he could help. And Gabe is survived by his parents, Ross and Emily, his brother, Ben, and his fiancée, Kelly, who he planned to marry next year. (Applause.)

And then there is nine-year-old Christina Taylor Green. Christina was an A student; she was a dancer; she was a gymnast; she was a swimmer. She decided that she wanted to be the first woman to play in the Major Leagues, and as the only girl on her Little League team, no one put it past her. (Applause.)

She showed an appreciation for life uncommon for a girl her age. She'd remind her mother, "We are so blessed. We have the best life." And she'd pay those blessings back by participating in a charity that helped children who were less fortunate.

Our hearts are broken by their sudden passing. Our hearts are broken — and yet, our hearts also have reason for fullness.

Our hearts are full of hope and thanks for the 13 Americans who survived the shooting, including the congresswoman many of them went to see on Saturday.

I have just come from the University Medical Center, just a mile from here, where our friend Gabby courageously fights to recover even as we speak. And I want to tell you — her husband Mark is here and he allows me to share this with you — right after we went to visit, a few minutes after we left her room and some of her colleagues in Congress were in the room, Gabby opened her eyes for the first time. (Applause.) Gabby opened her eyes for the first time. (Applause.)

Gabby opened her eyes. Gabby opened her eyes, so I can tell you she knows we are here. She knows we love her. And she knows that we are rooting for her through what is undoubtedly going to be a difficult journey. We are there for her. (Applause.)

Our hearts are full of thanks for that good news, and our hearts are full of gratitude for those who saved others. We are grateful to Daniel Hernandez — (applause) — a volunteer in Gabby's office. (Applause.)

And, Daniel, I'm sorry, you may deny it, but we've decided you are a hero because — (applause) — you ran through the chaos to minister to your boss, and tended to her wounds and helped keep her alive. (Applause.)

We are grateful to the men who tackled the gunman as he stopped to reload. (Applause.) Right over there. (Applause.) We are grateful for petite Patricia Maisch, who wrestled away the killer's ammunition, and undoubtedly saved some lives. (Applause.) And we are grateful for the doctors and nurses and first responders who worked wonders to heal those who'd been hurt. We are grateful to them. (Applause.)

**Specification:** These men and women remind us that heroism is found not only on the fields of battle. They remind us that heroism does not require special training or physical strength. Heroism is here, in the hearts of so many of our fellow citizens, all around us, just waiting to be summoned — as it was on Saturday morning. Their actions, their selflessness poses a challenge to each of us. It raises a question of what, beyond prayers and expressions of concern, is required of us going forward. How can we honor the fallen? How can we be true to their memory?

**Construction:** You see, when a tragedy like this strikes, it is part of our nature to demand explanations — to try and pose some order on the chaos and make sense out of that which seems senseless. Already we've seen a national conversation commence, not only about the motivations behind these killings, but about everything from the merits of gun safety laws to the adequacy of our mental health system. And much of this process, of debating what might be done to prevent such tragedies in the future, is an essential ingredient in our exercise of self-government.

But at a time when our discourse has become so sharply polarized — at a time when we are far too eager to lay the blame for all that ails the world at the feet of those who happen to think differently than we do — it's important for us to pause for a moment and make sure that we're talking with each other in a way that heals, not in a way that wounds. (Applause.)

Scripture tells us that there is evil in the world, and that terrible things happen for reasons that defy human understanding. In the words of Job, "When I looked for light, then came darkness." Bad things happen, and we have to guard against simple explanations in the aftermath.

For the truth is none of us can know exactly what triggered this vicious attack. None of us can know with any certainty what might have stopped these shots from being fired, or what thoughts lurked in the inner recesses of a violent man's mind. Yes, we have to examine all the facts behind this tragedy. We cannot and will not be passive in the face of such violence. We should be willing to challenge old assumptions in order to lessen the prospects of such violence in the future. (Applause.) But what we cannot do is use this tragedy as one more occasion to turn on each other. (Applause.) That we cannot do. (Applause.) That we cannot do.

**Proof:** As we discuss these issues, let each of us do so with a good dose of humility. Rather than pointing fingers or assigning blame, let's use this occasion to expand our moral imaginations, to listen to each other more carefully, to sharpen our instincts for empathy and remind ourselves of all the ways that our hopes and dreams are bound together. (Applause.)

After all, that's what most of us do when we lose somebody in our family — especially if the loss is unexpected. We're shaken out of our routines. We're forced to look inward. We reflect on the past: Did we spend enough time with an aging parent, we wonder. Did we express our gratitude for all the sacrifices that they made for us? Did we tell a spouse just how desperately we loved them, not just once in a while but every single day?

So sudden loss causes us to look backward — but it also forces us to look forward; to reflect on the present and the future, on the manner in which we live our lives and nurture our relationships with those who are still with us. (Applause.)

We may ask ourselves if we've shown enough kindness and generosity and compassion to the people in our lives. Perhaps we question whether we're doing right by our children, or our community, whether our priorities are in order.

We recognize our own mortality, and we are reminded that in the fleeting time we have on this Earth, what matters is not wealth, or status, or power, or fame — but rather, how well we have loved — (applause)— and what small part we have played in making the lives of other people better. (Applause.)

And that process — that process of reflection, of making sure we align our values with our actions — that, I believe, is what a tragedy like this requires.

For those who were harmed, those who were killed — they are part of our family, an American family 300 million strong. (Applause.) We may not have known them personally, but surely we see ourselves in them. In George and Dot, in Dorwan and Mavy, we sense the abiding love we have for our own husbands, our own wives, our own life partners. Phyllis — she's our mom or our grandma; Gabe our brother or son. (Applause.) In Judge Roll, we recognize not only a man who prized his family and doing his job well, but also a man who embodied America's fidelity to the law. (Applause.)

And in Gabby — in Gabby, we see a reflection of our public-spiritedness; that desire to participate in that sometimes frustrating, sometimes contentious, but always necessary and never-ending process to form a more perfect union. (Applause.)

And in Christina — in Christina we see all of our children. So curious, so trusting, so energetic, so full of magic. So deserving of our love. And so deserving of our good example.

If this tragedy prompts reflection and debate — as it should — let's make sure it's worthy of those we have lost. **(Applause.)** Let's make sure it's not on the usual plane of politics and point-scoring and pettiness that drifts away in the next news cycle.

The loss of these wonderful people should make every one of us strive to be better. To be better in our private lives, to be better friends and neighbors and coworkers and parents. And if, as has been discussed in recent days, their death helps usher in more civility in our public discourse, let us remember it is not because a simple lack of civility caused this tragedy — it did not — but rather because only a more civil and honest public discourse can help us face up to the challenges of our nation in a way that would make them proud. **(Applause.)**

We should be civil because we want to live up to the example of public servants like John Roll and Gabby Giffords, who knew first and foremost that we are all Americans, and that we can question each other's ideas without questioning each other's love of country and that our task, working together, is to constantly widen the circle of our concern so that we bequeath the American Dream to future generations. **(Applause.)**

They believed — they believed, and I believe that we can be better. Those who died here, those who saved life here — they help me believe. We may not be able to stop all evil in the world, but I know that how we treat one another, that's entirely up to us. **(Applause.)**

And I believe that for all our imperfections, we are full of decency and goodness, and that the forces that divide us are not as strong as those that unite us. **(Applause.)**

**Conclusion:** That's what I believe, in part because that's what a child like Christina Taylor Green believed. **(Applause.)**

Imagine — imagine for a moment, here was a young girl who was just becoming aware of our democracy; just beginning to understand the obligations of citizenship; just starting to glimpse the fact that some day she, too, might play a part in shaping her nation's future. She had been elected to her student council. She saw public service as something exciting and hopeful. She was off to meet her congresswoman, someone she was sure was good and important and might be a role model. She saw all this through the eyes of a child, undimmed by the cynicism or vitriol that we adults all too often just take for granted.

I want to live up to her expectations. (Applause.) I want our democracy to be as good as Christina imagined it. I want America to be as good as she imagined it. (Applause.) All of us — we should do everything we can to make sure this country lives up to our children's expectations. (Applause.)

As has already been mentioned, Christina was given to us on September 11th, 2001, one of 50 babies born that day to be pictured in a book called "Faces of Hope." On either side of her photo in that book were simple wishes for a child's life. "I hope you help those in need," read one. "I hope you know all the words to the National Anthem and sing it with your hand over your heart." (Applause.) "I hope you jump in rain puddles."

If there are rain puddles in Heaven, Christina is jumping in them today. (Applause.) And here on this Earth — here on this Earth, we place our hands over our hearts, and we commit ourselves as Americans to forging a country that is forever worthy of her gentle, happy spirit.

May God bless and keep those we've lost in restful and eternal peace. May He love and watch over the survivors. And may He bless the United States of America. (Applause.)

## 19.4 OSAMA BIN LADEN IS DEAD

May 1, 2011

**Enunciation:** THE PRESIDENT: [Given] Good evening. Tonight, I can report to the American people and to the world that the United States has conducted an operation that killed Osama bin Laden, the leader of al Qaeda, and a terrorist who's responsible for the murder of thousands of innocent men, women, and children.

It was nearly 10 years ago that a bright September day was darkened by the worst attack on the American people in our history. The images of 9/11 are seared into our national memory — hijacked planes cutting through a cloudless September sky; the Twin Towers collapsing to the ground; black smoke billowing up from the Pentagon; the wreckage of Flight 93 in Shanksville, Pennsylvania, where the actions of heroic citizens saved even more heartbreak and destruction.

And yet we know that the worst images are those that were unseen to the world. The empty seat at the dinner table. Children who were forced to grow up without their mother or their father. Parents who would never know the feeling of their child's embrace. Nearly 3,000 citizens taken from us, leaving a gaping hole in our hearts.

On September 11, 2001, in our time of grief, the American people came together. We offered our neighbors a hand, and we offered the wounded our blood. We reaffirmed our ties to each other, and our love of community and country. On that day, no matter where we came from, what God we prayed to, or what race or ethnicity we were, we were united as one American family.

We were also united in our resolve to protect our nation and to bring those who committed this vicious attack to justice. We quickly learned that the 9/11 attacks were carried out by al Qaeda — an organization headed by Osama bin Laden, which had openly declared war on the United States and was committed to killing innocents in our country and around the globe. [**Sought**] And so we went to war against al Qaeda to protect our citizens, our friends, and our allies.

**Exposition:** Over the last 10 years, thanks to the tireless and heroic work of our military and our counterterrorism professionals, we've made great strides in that effort. We've disrupted terrorist attacks and strengthened our homeland defense. In Afghanistan, we removed the Taliban government, which had given bin Laden and al Qaeda safe haven and support. And around the globe, we worked with our friends and allies to capture or kill scores of al Qaeda terrorists, including several who were a part of the 9/11 plot.

Yet Osama bin Laden avoided capture and escaped across the Afghan border into Pakistan. Meanwhile, al Qaeda continued to operate from along that border and operate through its affiliates across the world.

**Specification:** And so shortly after taking office, I directed Leon Panetta, the director of the CIA, to make the killing or capture of bin Laden the top priority of our war against al Qaeda, even as we continued our broader efforts to disrupt, dismantle, and defeat his network.

**Construction:** Then, last August, after years of painstaking work by our intelligence community, I was briefed on a possible lead to bin Laden. It was far from certain, and it took many months to run this thread to ground. I met repeatedly with my national security team as we developed more information about the possibility that we had located bin Laden hiding within a compound deep inside of Pakistan. And finally, last week, I determined that we had enough intelligence to take action, and authorized an operation to get Osama bin Laden and bring him to justice.

Today, at my direction, the United States launched a targeted operation against that compound in Abbottabad, Pakistan. A small team of Americans carried out the operation with extraordinary courage and capability. No Americans were harmed. They took care to avoid civilian casualties. After a firefight, they killed Osama bin Laden and took custody of his body.

For over two decades, bin Laden has been al Qaeda's leader and symbol, and has continued to plot attacks against our country and our friends and allies. The death of bin Laden marks the most significant achievement to date in our nation's effort to defeat al Qaeda.

**Proof:** Yet his death does not mark the end of our effort. There's no doubt that al Qaeda will continue to pursue attacks against us. We must — and we will — remain vigilant at home and abroad.

As we do, we must also reaffirm that the United States is not — and never will be — at war with Islam. I've made clear, just as President Bush did shortly after 9/11, that our war is not against Islam. Bin Laden was not a Muslim leader; he was a mass murderer of Muslims. Indeed, al Qaeda has slaughtered scores of Muslims in many countries, including our own. So his demise should be welcomed by all who believe in peace and human dignity.

Over the years, I've repeatedly made clear that we would take action within Pakistan if we knew where bin Laden was. That is what we've done. But it's important to note that our counterterrorism cooperation with Pakistan helped lead us to bin Laden and the compound where he was hiding. Indeed, bin Laden had declared war against Pakistan as well, and ordered attacks against the Pakistani people.

Tonight, I called President Zardari, and my team has also spoken with their Pakistani counterparts. They agree that this is a good and historic day for both of our nations. And going forward, it is essential that Pakistan continue to join us in the fight against al Qaeda and its affiliates.

The American people did not choose this fight. It came to our shores, and started with the senseless slaughter of our citizens. After nearly 10 years of service, struggle, and sacrifice, we know well the costs of war. These efforts weigh on me every time I, as Commander-in-Chief, have to sign a letter to a family that has lost a loved one, or look into the eyes of a service member who's been gravely wounded.

So Americans understand the costs of war. Yet as a country, we will never tolerate our security being threatened, nor stand idly by when our people have been killed.

We will be relentless in defense of our citizens and our friends and allies. We will be true to the values that make us who we are. And on nights like this one, we can say to those families who have lost loved ones to al Qaeda's terror: Justice has been done.

**Conclusion:** Tonight, we give thanks to the countless intelligence and counterterrorism professionals who've worked tirelessly to achieve this outcome. The American people do not see their work, nor know their names. But tonight, they feel the satisfaction of their work and the result of their pursuit of justice.

We give thanks for the men who carried out this operation, for they exemplify the professionalism, patriotism, and unparalleled courage of those who serve our country. And they are part of a generation that has borne the heaviest share of the burden since that September day.

Finally, let me say to the families who lost loved ones on 9/11 that we have never forgotten your loss, nor wavered in our commitment to see that we do whatever it takes to prevent another attack on our shores.

And tonight, let us think back to the sense of unity that prevailed on 9/11. I know that it has, at times, frayed. Yet today's achievement is a testament to the greatness of our country and the determination of the American people.

The cause of securing our country is not complete. But tonight, we are once again reminded that America can do whatever we set our mind to. That is the story of our history, whether it's the pursuit of prosperity for our people, or the struggle for equality for all our citizens; our commitment to stand up for our values abroad, and our sacrifices to make the world a safer place.

Let us remember that we can do these things not just because of wealth or power, but because of who we are: one nation, under God, indivisible, with liberty and justice for all.

Thank you. May God bless you. And may God bless the United States of America.

## 19.5 Michelle Obama, Democratic National Convention

Philadelphia, Pennsylvania, July 25, 2016

**Enunciation: [Given]** Thank you all. (Applause.) Thank you so much. You know, it's hard to believe that it has been eight years since I first came to this convention to talk with you about why I thought my husband should be President. (Applause.) Remember how I told you about his character and conviction, his decency and his grace — the traits that we've seen every day that he's served our country in the White House.

I also told you about our daughters — how they are the heart of our hearts, the center of our world. And during our time in the White House, we've had the joy of watching them grow from bubbly little girls into poised young women — a journey that started soon after we arrived in Washington, when they set off for their first day at their new school.

I will never forget that winter morning as I watched our girls, just seven and ten years old, pile into those black SUVs with all those big men with guns. (Laughter.) And I saw their little faces pressed up against the window, and the only thing I could think was, "What have we done?" (Laughter.) **[Sought]** See, because at that moment, I realized that our time in the White House would form the foundation for who they would become, and how well we managed this experience could truly make or break them.

**Exposition:** That is what Barack and I think about every day as we try to guide and protect our girls through the challenges of this unusual life in the spotlight — how we urge them to ignore those who question their father's citizenship or faith. (Applause.) How we insist that the hateful language they hear from public figures on TV does not represent the true spirit of this country. (Applause.) How we explain that when someone is cruel, or acts like a bully, you don't stoop to their level — no, our motto is, when they go low, we go high. (Applause.)

With every word we utter, with every action we take, we know our kids are watching us. We as parents are their most important role models. And let me tell you, Barack and I take that same approach to our jobs as President and First Lady, because we know that our words and actions matter not just to our girls, but to children across this country — kids who tell us, "I saw you on TV, I wrote a report on you for school." Kids like the little black boy who looked up at my husband, his eyes wide with hope, and he wondered, "Is my hair like yours?" (Applause.)

**Specification:** And make no mistake about it, this November, when we go to the polls, that is what we're deciding — not Democrat or Republican, not left or right. No, this election, and every election, is about who will have the power to shape our children for the next four or eight years of their lives. (Applause.) And I am here tonight because in this election, there is only one person who I trust with that responsibility, only one person who I believe is truly qualified to be President of the United States, and that is our friend, Hillary Clinton. (Applause.)

**Construction:** See, I trust Hillary to lead this country because I've seen her lifelong devotion to our nation's children — not just her own daughter, who she has raised to perfection — (applause) — but every child who needs a champion: Kids who take the long way to school to avoid the gangs. Kids who wonder how they'll ever afford college. Kids whose parents don't speak a word of English but dream of a better life. Kids who look to us to determine who and what they can be.

You see, Hillary has spent decades doing the relentless, thankless work to actually make a difference in their lives — (applause) — advocating for kids with disabilities as a young lawyer. Fighting for children's health care as First Lady and for quality child care in the Senate. And when she didn't win the nomination eight years ago, she didn't get angry or disillusioned. (Applause.) Hillary did not pack up and go home. Because as a true public servant, Hillary knows that this is so much bigger than her own desires and disappointments. (Applause.) So she proudly stepped up to serve our country once again as Secretary of State, traveling the globe to keep our kids safe.

And look, there were plenty of moments when Hillary could have decided that this work was too hard, that the price of public service was too high, that she was tired of being picked apart for how she looks or how she talks or even how she laughs. But here's the thing — what I admire most about Hillary is that she never buckles under pressure. (Applause.) She never takes the easy way out. And Hillary Clinton has never quit on anything in her life. (Applause.)

**Proof:** And when I think about the kind of President that I want for my girls and all our children, that's what I want. I want someone with the proven strength to persevere. Someone who knows this job and takes it seriously. Someone who understands that the issues a President faces are not black and white and cannot be boiled down to 140 characters. (Applause.) Because when you have the nuclear codes at your fingertips and the military in your command, you can't make snap decisions. You can't have a thin skin or a tendency to lash out. You need to be steady, and measured, and well-informed. (Applause.)

I want a President with a record of public service, someone whose life's work shows our children that we don't chase fame and fortune for ourselves, we fight to give everyone a chance to succeed — (applause) — and we give back, even when we're struggling ourselves, because we know that there is always someone worse off, and there but for the grace of God go I. (Applause.)

I want a President who will teach our children that everyone in this country matters — a President who truly believes in the vision that our founders put forth all those years ago: That we are all created equal, each a beloved part of the great American story. (Applause.) And when crisis hits, we don't turn against each other — no, we listen to each other. We lean on each other. Because we are always stronger together. (Applause.)

And I am here tonight because I know that that is the kind of president that Hillary Clinton will be. And that's why, in this election, I'm with her. (Applause.)

You see, Hillary understands that the President is about one thing and one thing only — it's about leaving something better for our kids. That's how we've always moved this country forward — by all of us coming together on behalf of our children — folks who volunteer to coach that team, to teach that Sunday school class because they know it takes a village. Heroes of every color and creed who wear the uniform and risk their lives to keep passing down those blessings of liberty.

Police officers and protestors in Dallas who all desperately want to keep our children safe. (Applause.) People who lined up in Orlando to donate blood because it could have been their son, their daughter in that club. (Applause.) Leaders like Tim Kaine — (applause) — who show our kids what decency and devotion look like. Leaders like Hillary Clinton, who has the guts and the grace to keep coming back and putting those cracks in that highest and hardest glass ceiling until she finally breaks through, lifting all of us along with her. (Applause.)

That is the story of this country, the story that has brought me to this stage tonight, the story of generations of people who felt the lash of bondage, the shame of servitude, the sting of segregation, but who kept on striving and hoping and doing what needed to be done so that today, I wake up every morning in a house that was built by slaves — (applause) — and I watch my daughters — two beautiful, intelligent, black young women — playing with their dogs on the White House lawn. (Applause.) And because of Hillary Clinton, my daughters — and all our sons and daughters — now take for granted that a woman can be President of the United States. (Applause.)

**Conclusion:** So don't let anyone ever tell you that this country isn't great, that somehow we need to make it great again. Because this, right now, is the greatest country on earth. (Applause.) And as my daughters prepare to set out into the world, I want a leader who is worthy of that truth, a leader who is worthy of my girls' promise and all our kids' promise, a leader who will be guided every day by the love and hope and impossibly big dreams that we all have for our children.

So in this election, we cannot sit back and hope that everything works out for the best. We cannot afford to be tired, or frustrated, or cynical. No, hear me — between now and November, we need to do what we did eight years ago and four years ago: We need to knock on every door. We need to get out every vote. We need to pour every last ounce of our passion and our strength and our love for this country into electing Hillary Clinton as President of the United States of America.

Let's get to work. Thank you all, and God bless.

# A LANGUAGE OF SCIENCE
# FOR HUMAN ISSUES

The six elements of a proposition are a "verbal" scientific method for human problems. In 1969, Professor Glenn Morrow, who translated Proclus' commentary on Euclid's *Elements*, opined:

> Among the many creations of the Greek mind, Greek geometry is one of the most splendid, and Euclid has been its honored exponent and spokesman for more than two thousand years. Yet the respect universally accorded him and the science he stands for is seldom accompanied by an understanding of the intellectual principles on which this science was built and the procedures by which its details were developed.[1]

Prior to Thomas Jefferson drafting the Declaration of Independence, John Adams said to him, "You can write ten times better than I can."[2] Adams commented, "...I had a great Opinion of the Elegance of his pen and none at all of my own."[3]

Decades after Adams and Jefferson died, William Herndon described Abraham Lincoln's study of Euclid. Herndon set a scene of Judge and attorneys riding the Illinois Eighth Circuit from courthouse to courthouse four to six months during the spring and fall:[4]

> Placing a candle on a chair at the head of the bed, he [Lincoln] would read and study for hours. I have known him to study in this position till two o'clock in the morning. Meanwhile, I and others who chanced to occupy the same room would be safely and soundly asleep.

> On the circuit in this way he studied Euclid until he could with ease demonstrate all the propositions in the six books. How he could maintain his mental equilibrium or concentrate his thoughts on an abstract mathematical proposition, while [Judge David] Davis, [Stephen T.] Logan, [Leonard] Swett, [Benjamin] Edwards, and I so industriously and volubly filled the air with our interminable snoring was a problem none of us could ever solve.[5]

Lincoln's goal was not to entertain; it was to convince.[6] Attorney Henry Clay Whitney, who rode the circuit with Lincoln, wrote:

> I once knew of his [Lincoln] making a pupil of a hostler [horse caretaker] in his study of Euclid on the circuit. He did not, like Archimedes, run through the

streets crying "Eureka!" but he was so joyous at his geometrical lesson that he must share his happiness, even though he could find no better auditor than a stableman.[7]

We will never know the details of Lincoln's eureka moment. We know steady improvement results from internalizing the six elements of a proposition. Jefferson and Lincoln put candlelight on the road. Once you see the road, you can walk it. With eyes open, there is no limit to where you can go and what you can achieve. Civility and the science of persuasion are yours.

The elements extend the power of human reason. The six elements boosted Thomas Jefferson's writing skill to ten times that of Adams. With just one year of formal education, Abraham Lincoln persuaded his way into the White House, and led the nation through perilous times. Not every problem can be solved. Civility, facts, and logic increase the odds. The six-element path is a road of reason.

Proclus demarcated Euclid's Proposition 1 over 1500 years ago. Proclus' demarcation of Proposition 1 appears on pages 70 and 71. Proclus provided commentary on the demarcation. The language within quotation marks is Proclus' representation of Euclid's Proposition 1; the unquoted text is Proclus' commentary:

> In this case the enunciation consists of both what is given and what is sought. What is given is a finite straight line, and what is sought is how to construct an equilateral triangle on it. The statement of the given precedes and the statement of what is sought follows, so that we may weave them together as "If there is a finite straight line, it is possible to construct an equilateral triangle on it." If there were no straight line, no triangle could be produced, for a triangle is bounded by straight lines; nor could it if the line were not finite, for an angle can be constructed only at a definite point, and an unbounded line has no end point.
>
> Next after the enunciation is the exposition: "Let this be the given finite line." You see that the exposition itself mentions only the given, without reference to what is sought.
>
> Upon this follows the specification: "It is required to construct an equilateral triangle on the designated finite straight line." In a sense the purpose of the specification is to fix our attention; it makes us more attentive to the proof by announcing what is to be proved, just as the exposition puts us in a better position for learning by producing the given element before our eyes.
>
> After the specification comes the construction: "Let a circle be described with center at one extremity of the line and the remainder of the line as distance; again let a circle be described with the other extremity as center and the same distance as before; and then from the point of intersection of the circles let straight lines be

joined to the two extremities of the given straight line." You observe that for the construction I make use of the two postulates that a straight line may be drawn from any point to any other and that a circle may be described with [any] center and distance. In general the postulates are contributory to constructions and the axioms to proofs.

Next comes the proof: "Since one of the two points on the given straight line is the center of the circle enclosing it, the line drawn to the point of intersection is equal to the given straight line. For the same reason, since the other point on the given straight line is itself the center of the circle enclosing it, the line drawn from it to the point of intersection is equal to the given straight line." These inferences are suggested to us by the definition of the circle, which says that all the lines drawn from its center are equal. "Each of these lines is therefore equal to the same line; and things equal to the same thing are equal to each other" by the first axiom. "The three lines therefore are equal, and an equilateral triangle [ABC] has been constructed on this given straight line." This is the first conclusion following upon the exposition.

And then comes the general conclusion: "An equilateral triangle has therefore been constructed upon the given straight line." For even if you make the line double that set forth in the exposition, or triple, or of any other length greater or less than it, the same construction and proof would fit it. [color and paragraphing added][8]

## QUESTIONS

ONE: What is the weakness in Proclus' Proposition 1 **Exposition** commentary ?

TWO: What might explain lack of depth in Proclus' commentary on Proposition 1's **Exposition**? What is its strength?

THREE: Why do the six elements work in speeches and writings?

The elements work because the six elements of a proposition that were used to demonstrate theorems or problems of plane geometry in the first six books of Euclid are word-based, not algebraic. Words, not algebra, proved Euclid's assembled theorems and problems. Abraham Lincoln studied the first six books of Euclid. Lincoln in speeches and letters then applied the same elements to human problems: Slavery, Civil War, and preserving the Union.

Lincoln's six-element verbal structure conveyed iron logic. By civilly convincing, instead of entertaining, shouting naked conclusions, or parroting soundbites, Lincoln persuaded a nation to end slavery. Earlier Thomas Jefferson used the same method to persuade a nation to declare independence.

# Endnotes

## Conventions

1. Malone, *The Story of the Declaration of Independence*, 87.

## Introduction

1. Rabbi Shalom Arush, *The Garden of Emuna*, 13.
2. Arnold, "Reminiscences of the Illinois Bar: 1840 – Lincoln and Douglas as Orators and Lawyers," *Illinois Bar Journal* 47 (1959): 577.
3. Hirsch and Van Haften, *The Ultimate Guide to the Gettysburg Address*.
4. Hirsch and Van Haften, *The Ultimate Guide to the Declaration of Independence*.
5. Proclus, *A Commentary on the First Book of Euclid's Elements*, 159.
6. United States Continental Congress, "Tuesday, June 11, 1776," *Journals of the Continental Congress*, 431; Adams, *Diary and Autobiography of John Adams*, 3:393.
7. Adams, "To Timothy Pickering, August 6, 1822," *The Works of John Adams, Second President of the United States*, 2:514.
8. Lehmann, *Thomas Jefferson: American Humanist*, 36; Cunningham, *Jefferson vs. Hamilton: Confrontations that Shaped a Nation*, 3; Parton, *Life of Thomas Jefferson*, 30.
9. Lincoln, "Brief Autobiography, June, 1858," *Collected Works*, 2:459; Lincoln, "Autobiography Written for John L. Scripps, June, 1860," *Collected Works*, 4:62.
10. Hirsch and Van Haften, *Abraham Lincoln and the Structure of Reason*, 23, 43.
11. Hirsch and Van Haften, *Abraham Lincoln and the Structure of Reason*; Lincoln, "Autobiography Written for John L. Scripps, June, 1860," *Collected Works*, 4:62.
12. Lincoln, "Mr. Lincoln's Rejoinder, Fourth Debate with Stephen A. Douglas at Charleston, Illinois, September 18, 1858," *Collected Works*, 3:186.
13. The Thomas Jefferson Papers, "Autobiography Draft Fragment, January 6 through July 27, 1821," The Library of Congress, www.loc.gov/item/mtjbib024000 (accessed March 9, 2016); Jefferson, *The Autobiography of Thomas Jefferson*, 40.
14. Proclus, *A Commentary on the First Book of Euclid's Elements*, 159.
15. Proclus, *A Commentary on the First Book of Euclid's Elements*, 159.
16. Lucas Siorvanes, "Proclus," Oxford Bibliographies, www.oxfordbibliographies.com/view/document/obo-9780195389661/obo-9780195389661-0157.xml;jsessionid=C72370AC47815861BB864052161AAECE, accessed April 23, 2017).
17. Proclus, *A Commentary on the First Book of Euclid's Elements*, 159.
18. Hirsch and Van Haften, *Abraham Lincoln and the Structure of Reason*, 29.
19. Proclus, *A Commentary on the First Book of Euclid's Elements*, 159.
20. Hirsch and Van Haften, *Abraham Lincoln and the Structure of Reason*, 29.
21. Proclus, *A Commentary on the First Book of Euclid's Elements*, 159.
22. Hirsch and Van Haften, *Abraham Lincoln and the Structure of Reason*, 29.
23. Proclus, *A Commentary on the First Book of Euclid's Elements*, 159.
24. Hirsch and Van Haften, *Abraham Lincoln and the Structure of Reason*, 29.
25. Proclus, *A Commentary on the First Book of Euclid's Elements*, 159.
26. Hirsch and Van Haften, *Abraham Lincoln and the Structure of Reason*, 29.
27. Proclus, *A Commentary on the First Book of Euclid's Elements*, 159.
28. Hirsch and Van Haften, *Abraham Lincoln and the Structure of Reason*, 29.
29. Angle, "Robert Todd Lincoln to Isaac Markens, June 18, 1918," *A Portrait of Abraham Lincoln in Letters by His Oldest Son*, 62.
30. Wilson, *Lincoln's Sword: The Presidency and the Power of Words*, 45.
31. Strunk and White, *The Elements of Style*, 71; Garner, *The Chicago Guide to Grammar, Usage, and Punctuation*, 70.
32. Jefferson, "To Thomas Jefferson Randolph, December 7, 1808," *Papers of the Randolph, Jefferson, Eppes, Nicholas and Kean families, 1785-1865*, Accession #2143, Special Collections, University of Virginia Library, Charlottesville, VA.
33. Jefferson, "To Joseph C. Cabell, September 9, 1817," *The Papers of Thomas Jefferson: Retirement Series*, 12:15-16.
34. Looney, *The Papers of Thomas Jefferson: Retirement Series*, 1:106.
35. The Thomas Jefferson Papers, "Horatio G. Spafford to Thomas Jefferson, February 28, 1822," The Library of Congress, www.loc.gov/item/mtjbib024310/ (accessed September 8, 2016).

36. The Thomas Jefferson Papers, "Thomas Jefferson to Horatio G. Spafford, March 19, 1822," The Library of Congress, www.loc.gov/item/mtjbib024324/ (accessed September 8, 2016).

37. In late December 2010, shortly after *Abraham Lincoln and the Structure of Reason* was published, Dan Van Haften was signing books at a Borders near the White House. A Borders executive suggested Dan get a copy of *Abraham Lincoln and the Structure of Reason* to President Obama. Dan said he would like to do that, but didn't know how. The Borders executive said, "I do." The Borders executive knew the White House librarian. A few weeks later President Obama was using the six elements of a proposition to structure speeches. See *Barack Obama, Abraham Lincoln, and the Structure of Reason*. Former Speaker of the U.S. House of Representatives Newt Gingrich discovered *Abraham Lincoln and the Structure of Reason,* before David Hirsch presented a copy to him. *Cf.* www.thestructureofreason.com/you-can-do-this/speakers-only (accessed February 21, 2016).

38. Jefferson, "To John Adams, October 14, 1816," *The Papers of Thomas Jefferson: Retirement Series*, 10:460.

39. Jefferson, "To William Duane, July 3, 1814," *The Papers of Thomas Jefferson: Retirement Series,* 7:450; Jefferson, *A Treatise on Political Economy, by the Count Destutt Tracy* .

40. Jefferson, "To Joseph Milligan, October 25, 1818," *The Papers of Thomas Jefferson: Retirement Series,* 13:336.

41. Chase, *The Tyranny of Words*, 3.

42. Chase, *The Tyranny of Words*, 144-145.

43. Chase, *The Tyranny of Words*, 142-144.

44. Chase, *The Tyranny of Words*, 356.

45. Chase, *The Tyranny of Words*, 356-359.

46. Chase, *The Tyranny of Words*, 359-360; Hogben, *Mathematics for the Million*, 641.

## Lesson 1: Enunciation: Why Are We Here?

1. Proclus, *A Commentary on the First Book of Euclid's Elements,* 159.

2. Lincoln, "Address Delivered at the Dedication of the Cemetery at Gettysburg, Final Text, November 19, 1863," *Collected Works*, 7:23.

3. Jefferson, "To John Stockdale, February 1, 1787," *The Papers of Thomas Jefferson*, 11:107-108.

4. Jefferson, "To Henry Dearborn, February 18, 1801," *The Papers of Thomas Jefferson*, 33:13.

5. Jefferson, "To Mary Jefferson Eppes, March 3, 1802," *The Papers of Thomas Jefferson*, 36:676-677.

6. Jefferson, "To Tunis Wortman, August 15, 1813," *The Papers of Thomas Jefferson: Retirement Series*, 6:400-401.

7. Lincoln, "To George Robertson, August 15, 1855," *The Collected Works of Abraham Lincoln*, 2:317-318.

8. Lincoln, "To Samuel C. Davis and Company, November 17, 1858," *The Collected Works of Abraham Lincoln*, 3:338.

9. Lincoln, "To David Hunter, October 24, 1861," *The Collected Works of Abraham Lincoln*, 5:1-2.

10. Proclus, *A Commentary on the First Book of Euclid's Elements,* 162-164.

11. Euclid, *The Thirteen Books of Euclid's Elements, Translated from the Text of Heiberg with Introduction and Commentary by Sir Thomas L. Heath, Volume I* (New York, NY: Dover Publications, Inc., 1956), 241.

## Lesson 2: Exposition: What Needs to be Investigated?

1. Proclus, *A Commentary on the First Book of Euclid's Elements,* 159.

2. Lincoln, "Address Delivered at the Dedication of the Cemetery at Gettysburg, Final Text, November 19, 1863," *Collected Works*, 7:23.

## Lesson 3: Specification: The Hypothesis

1. Proclus, *A Commentary on the First Book of Euclid's Elements,* 159.

2. Lincoln, "Address Delivered at the Dedication of the Cemetery at Gettysburg, Final Text, November 19, 1863," *Collected Works*, 7:23.

## Lesson 4: Construction: Array the Evidence

1. Proclus, *A Commentary on the First Book of Euclid's Elements,* 159.

2. Lincoln, "Address Delivered at the Dedication of the Cemetery at Gettysburg, Final Text, November 19, 1863," *Collected Works*, 7:23.

3. See Abraham Lincoln, "Mr. Lincoln's Rejoinder, Fourth Debate with Stephen A. Douglas at Charleston, Illinois, September 18, 1858," *Collected Works,* 3:186.

## Lesson 5: Proof: Confirm the Proposed Inference

1. Proclus, *A Commentary on the First Book of Euclid's Elements,* 159.
2. Lincoln, "Address Delivered at the Dedication of the Cemetery at Gettysburg, Final Text, November 19, 1863," *Collected Works,* 7:23.
3. See Abraham Lincoln, "Mr. Lincoln's Rejoinder, Fourth Debate with Stephen A. Douglas at Charleston, Illinois, September 18, 1858,"*Collected Works*, 3:186.

## Lesson 6: Conclusion: What Was Demonstrated?

1. Proclus, *A Commentary on the First Book of Euclid's Elements,* 159.
2. Lincoln, "Address Delivered at the Dedication of the Cemetery at Gettysburg, Final Text, November 19, 1863," *Collected Works,* 7:23.
3. "Dearborn, Henry," *Biographical Directory of the United States Congress 1774-2005*, 937.
4. Hirsch and Van Haften, *Abraham Lincoln and the Structure of Reason*, 274.
5. Bacon and O'Hern, "Isaac Briggs (1763-1825) MSA SC 3520-15898", Archives of Maryland (Biographical Series), http://msa.maryland.gov/megafile/msa/speccol/sc3500/sc3520/015800/015898/html/15898bio.html (accessed February 24, 2018).
6. Peterson, *Visitors to Monticello*, 90.
7. The Thomas Jefferson Papers, "Thomas Jefferson to Frances Wright, August 7, 1825," The Library of Congress, www.loc.gov/resource/mtj1.055_0461_0462/ (accessed February 24, 2018).

## Lesson 7: The Method is the Message

1. McLuhan, *Understanding Media: The Extensions of Man*, 7-21.
2. See Proclus, *A Commentary on the First Book of Euclid's Elements,* 159.
3. Proclus, *A Commentary on the First Book of Euclid's Elements,* 159.
4. Lincoln, "Mr. Lincoln's Rejoinder, Fourth Debate with Stephen A. Douglas at Charleston, Illinois, September 18, 1858," *Collected Works*, 3:186.
5. Proclus, *A Commentary on the First Book of Euclid's Elements,* 159.
6. Proclus, *A Commentary on the First Book of Euclid's Elements,* 159.
7. Proclus, *A Commentary on the First Book of Euclid's Elements,* 159.
8. Proclus, *A Commentary on the First Book of Euclid's Elements,* 159.
9. Proclus, *A Commentary on the First Book of Euclid's Elements,* 159.
10. Proclus, *A Commentary on the First Book of Euclid's Elements,* 159.

## Lesson 8: What's in a Name?

1. Newkirk, *Lincoln Lessons for Today*, 63.
2. Herndon and Weik, *Herndon's Lincoln*, 193-194.
3. *See* Hirsch and Van Haften, *Abraham Lincoln and the Structure of Reason*, 23, 43.
4. Lincoln, "Autobiography Written for John L. Scripps, June, 1860," *Collected Works*, 4:62; Hirsch and Van Haften, *Abraham Lincoln and the Structure of Reason*, 26-30.
5. Hadley, "The Meaning and Purpose of Secondary Education", *The School Review*, Vol. X, No. 10, 738 (1902).
6. Gow, *A Short History of Greek Mathematics*, 199.
7. Heath, *A History of Greek Mathematics, Vol. I*, 370.
8. Maziarz and Greenwood, *Greek Mathematical Philosophy*, 248.
9. Proclus, *A Commentary on the First Book of Euclid's Elements,* 159.
10. Mueller, *Philosophy of Mathematics and Deductive Structure in Euclid's* Elements, 11.
11. Proclus, *A Commentary on the First Book of Euclid's Elements,* 159.
12. Proclus, *A Commentary on the First Book of Euclid's Elements,* 159.
13. Proclus, *A Commentary on the First Book of Euclid's Elements,* 159.
14. Proclus, *A Commentary on the First Book of Euclid's Elements,* 159.
15. Proclus, *A Commentary on the First Book of Euclid's Elements,* 159.
16. Proclus, *A Commentary on the First Book of Euclid's Elements,* 159.
17. Proclus, *A Commentary on the First Book of Euclid's Elements,* 159.
18. Allen, et al., *Geometry Student's Text, Part I*, 11.
19. *Jacobellis v. Ohio,* 378 U. S. 184, 197, 84 S.Ct. 1676, 1683, 12 L.Ed.2d 793, 804 (1964).

## Lesson 9: Letter to Ulysses S. Grant

1. See Proclus, *A Commentary on the First Book of Euclid's Elements*, 162-164.
2. Hirsch and Van Haften, *The Ultimate Guide to the Declaration of Independence*, 49.
3. Hirsch and Van Haften, *Barack Obama, Abraham Lincoln, and the Structure of Reason*.
4. One may also look back to the Exposition if help is needed finding the bottom edge of the Construction, and look back to the Specification for assistance identifying the same line from the top edge of the Proof.
5. Lincoln, "To Ulysses S. Grant, January 19, 1865," *Collected Works*, 8:223.

## Lesson 10: Lincoln's Farewell Address

1. Arnold, "Reminiscences of the Illinois Bar: 1840 – Lincoln and Douglas as Orators and Lawyers," *Illinois Bar Journal* 47 (1959): 577.
2. Lincoln, "Farewell Address at Springfield, Illinois [A. Version], February 11, 1861," *Collected Works*, 4:190.

## Lesson 11: The Investigation

1. Rankin, *Intimate Character Sketches of Abraham Lincoln*, 61.
2. Herndon and Weik, *Herndon's Lincoln*, 224.
3. Herndon and Weik, *Herndon's Lincoln*, 356-357.
4. Herndon and Weik, *Herndon's Lincoln*, 273-274.
5. Frank, *Lincoln as a Lawyer*, 138.
6. Rankin, *Personal Recollections of Abraham Lincoln*, 246; Holzer, *Lincoln at Cooper Union: The Speech that Made Abraham Lincoln President*, 32-33, 121.
7. Holzer, *Lincoln at Cooper Union: The Speech that Made Abraham Lincoln President*, 235-236.
8. Hirsch and Van Haften, *Abraham Lincoln and the Structure of Reason*, 33, 326-344.
9. Hirsch and Van Haften, "Appendix G: Address at Cooper Institute," *Abraham Lincoln and the Structure of Reason*, 326.
10. Hirsch and Van Haften, "Appendix G: Address at Cooper Institute," *Abraham Lincoln and the Structure of Reason*, 326-327.
11. Hirsch and Van Haften, "Appendix G: Address at Cooper Institute," *Abraham Lincoln and the Structure of Reason*, 327.
12. Hirsch and Van Haften, "Appendix G: Address at Cooper Institute," *Abraham Lincoln and the Structure of Reason*, 330.
13. Peters, "First Congress, Session I, Chapter I, Section 1.—An Act to regulate the Time and Manner of administering certain Oaths, June 1, 1789," *The Public Statutes at Large of the United States of America*, 1:23.
14. U.S Constitution, art. 2, sec. 1.
15. Lincoln's 1860 Address at Cooper Institute contained three propositions. The first proposition expanded on Stephen A. Douglas' position that the founders understood the Constitution better than we. Lincoln focused on Douglas' statement as though it were an admission. Lincoln added that surely a signer of the United States Constitution would not violate his oath of office to follow the Constitution. Cooper Union's first proposition collected facts regarding signer votes or actions that appeared to regulate slavery in the territories. Most of those facts were arrayed in the first proposition's Construction. Lincoln transformed the opposition's "admission" that the founders understood the question better than we, into a demonstration against Douglas's popular sovereignty position regarding introduction of slavery in the territories. Lincoln went out of his way to appear honest with the facts. Overlooked for more than 150 years is the fact Lincoln's math was off. Lincoln claimed 21 out of 38 founders voted for legislation that regulated slavery in the territories. The problem is that three of the 21 federal legislators so voted only under the Articles of Confederation. Two of those three votes were necessary for Lincoln to claim a majority. Lincoln counted all three. A vote pre-Constitution speaks nothing with respect to Constitutionality under the Constitution itself. In a brilliant demonstration, Lincoln was actually two votes short. On October 1, 2009, Harvard Professor John Stauffer, David Hirsch, and Dan Van Haften met in Hirsch's Des Moines law office. Professor Stauffer was presented a 99% complete, pre-publication draft manuscript of *Abraham Lincoln and the Structure of Reason*. Professor Stauffer carefully looked at Chapters Two (demonstration of the six elements of a proposition) and Three (Lincoln's deception regarding votes of the founders concerning regulating slavery in the northwest territories). He asked, "If Lincoln had been questioned on the 'logical deception' described in Chapter Three, could he have defended it?" Hirsch immediately responded yes, Lincoln could have defended it in a "wishy washy" way. Lincoln says in the Conclusion of the first Cooper Union proposition, "The sum of the whole is, that of our thirty-nine fathers who framed the original Constitution, twenty-one—a clear majority of the whole—certainly understood that no proper division of

local from federal authority, nor any part of the Constitution, forbade the Federal Government to control slavery in the federal territories; while all the rest probably had the same understanding. Such, unquestionably, was the understanding of our fathers who framed the original Constitution; and the text affirms that they understood the question 'better than we.'…It is surely safe to assume that the thirty-nine framers of the original Constitution, and the seventy-six members of the Congress which framed the amendments thereto, taken together, do certainly include those who may be fairly called 'our fathers who framed the Government under which we live.' And so assuming, I defy any man to show that any one of them ever, in his whole life, declared that, in his understanding, any proper division of local from federal authority, or any part of the Constitution, forbade the Federal Government to control as to slavery in the federal territories."

16. *Cf.* Hirsch and Van Haften, "Chapter 3: Honest Abe?," *Abraham Lincoln and the Structure of Reason*, 48-53.
17. Hirsch and Van Haften, "Appendix G: Address at Cooper Institute," *Abraham Lincoln and the Structure of Reason*, 327-330.
18. See Lincoln, "Mr. Lincoln's Rejoinder, Fourth Debate with Stephen A. Douglas at Charleston, Illinois, September 18, 1858," *Collected Works*, 3:186.
19. Hirsch and Van Haften, "Appendix G: Address at Cooper Institute," *Abraham Lincoln and the Structure of Reason*, 332.
20. Oldroyd, *The Lincoln Memorial: Album-Immortelles*, 535-536.
21. *Cf.* Chase, *The Tyranny of Words*, 359-360.

## Lesson 12: Writing

1. Herndon and Weik, *Herndon's Lincoln*, 197.
2. Literature & Latte, "Scrivener," www.literatureandlatte.com (accessed February 28, 2018).

## Lesson 13: General Principles

1. Lincoln, "Second Inaugural Address, March 4, 1865," *Collected Works*, 8:333.
2. Lincoln, "To Thurlow Weed, March 15, 1865," *Collected Works*, 8:356.
3. Jefferson, "To John Pintard, January 9, 1814," *The Papers of Thomas Jefferson: Retirement Series*, 7:119-120.
4. Jefferson, "To Samuel M. Burnside, January 9, 1814," *The Papers of Thomas Jefferson: Retirement Series*, 7:115.

## Lesson 14: Credibility is Everything

1. Lincoln, "Fourth Debate with Stephen A. Douglas at Charleston, Illinois, September 18, 1858," *Collected Works*, 3:186.
2. Looney, *The Papers of Thomas Jefferson: Retirement Series*, 5:473.
3. White, *A. Lincoln: A Biography*, 608-609.
4. Reid, "Newspaper Response to the Gettysburg Address," *Quarterly Journal of Speech* 53 (February 1967), 52.
5. Hirsch and Van Haften, "Appendix C: A House Divided," *Abraham Lincoln and the Structure of Reason*, 280.
6. Lincoln, "Speech at Peoria, Illinois, October 16, 1854," *Collected Works*, 2:247-283. For the Peoria speech demarcated into six major propositions, see see www.thestructureofreason.com/the-peoria-speech-unveiled.
7. Lincoln, "A House Divided, June 16, 1858," *Collected Works*, 2:461-469.
8. Lincoln, "Address at Cooper Institute, February 27, 1860," *Collected Works*, 3:522-550.
9. Lincoln, "First Inaugural Address—Final Text, March 4, 1861," *Collected Works*, 4:262-271.

## Lesson 16: Freedom

1. Wanamaker, *The Voice of Lincoln*, 130.
2. Malone, *The Story of the Declaration of Independence*, 86.
3. Jefferson, "The Declaration of Independence, July 4, 1776," *The Papers of Thomas Jefferson*, 1:429-432.
4. Jefferson, "82. A Bill for Establishing Religious Freedom," *The Papers of Thomas Jefferson*, 2:545-547.
5. The Thomas Jefferson Papers, "Autobiography Draft Fragment, January 6 through July 27, 1821," The Library of Congress, www.loc.gov/item/mtjbib024000 (accessed March 6, 2016); Jefferson, *The Autobiography of Thomas Jefferson*, 40.
6. Lincoln, "Address at Cooper Institute, New York City, February 27, 1860," *Collected Works*, 3:522-532.
7. Lincoln, "Second Inaugural Address, March 4, 1865," *Collected Works*, 8:332-333.

## Lesson 17: Demarcation Exercises

1. Patrick, "Brissot, Jean Pierre," *Chambers's Biographical Dictionary*, 134; Brissot de Warville, "To Thomas Jefferson, February 10, 1788," *The Papers of Thomas Jefferson*, 12:577.
2. Jefferson, "To Brissot de Warville, February 11, 1788," *The Papers of Thomas Jefferson*, 12:577-578.
3. Looney, *The Papers of Thomas Jefferson: Retirement Series*, 1:193-194.
4. Looney, *The Papers of Thomas Jefferson: Retirement Series*, 5:473.
5. Looney, *The Papers of Thomas Jefferson: Retirement Series*, 5:473.
6. Patterson, "From Robert Patterson, November 30, 1812," *The Papers of Thomas Jefferson: Retirement Series*, 5:471.
7. Jefferson, "To Robert Patterson, December 27, 1812," *The Papers of Thomas Jefferson: Retirement Series*, 5:506-507.
8. Giffords and Kelly, *Gabby: A Story of Courage and Hope*, 18, 21.
9. Obama, "Remarks by the President at a Memorial Service for the Victims of the Shooting in Tucson, Arizona," The White House Office of the Press Secretary, obamawhitehouse.archives.gov/the-press-office/2011/01/12/remarks-president-barack-obama-memorial-service-victims-shooting-tucson (accessed February 28, 2018).
10. Obama, "Remarks by the President on Osama Bin Laden," The White House Office of the Press Secretary, obamawhitehouse.archives.gov/the-press-office/2011/05/02/remarks-president-osama-bin-laden (accessed February 28 , 2018).
11. Michele Obama, "Remarks by the First Lady at the Democratic National Convention, Wells Fargo Center, Philadelphia, Pennsylvania," The White House Office of the Press Secretary, obamawhitehouse.archives.gov/the-press-office/2016/07/25/remarks-first-lady-democratic-national-convention (accessed February 28, 2018).

## Lesson 18: Hints for Demarcation Exercises

1. Niebuhr, "Obama's 'Gettysburg Moment': For Us, the Living," The Huffington Post, www.huffingtonpost.com/gustav-niebuhr/obamas-gettysburg-moment-_b_808524.html (accessed February 28, 2018); Hirsch and Van Haften, *Barack Obama, Abraham Lincoln, and the Structure of Reason*, 9.

## Lesson 20: A Language of Science for Human Issues

1. Proclus, *A Commentary on the First Book of Euclid's Elements*, xxxiii.
2. Adams, "To Timothy Pickering, August 6, 1822," *The Works of John Adams, Second President of the United States*, 2:514.
3. Adams, *Diary and Autobiography of John Adams*, 3:336.
4. See Miers, *Lincoln Day by Day: A Chronology 1809-1865*. When riding the circuit, Lincoln generally left Springfield around April 1, and again in late September.
5. Herndon and Weik, *Herndon's Lincoln*, 194.
6. Arnold, "Reminiscences of the Illinois Bar: 1840 – Lincoln and Douglas as Orators and Lawyers," *Illinois Bar Journal* 47 (1959): 577.
7. Whitney, *Lincoln the Citizen*, 43.
8. Proclus, *A Commentary on the First Book of Euclid's Elements,* 162-164.

# BIBLIOGRAPHY

Archival Sources

University of Virginia Library
Papers of the Randolph, Jefferson, Eppes, Nicholas and Kean families, 1785-1865.


Electronic Sources (Internet)

Bacon, Kyle, and Megan O'Hern. "Isaac Briggs (1763-1825) MSA SC 3520-15898."
    Archives of Maryland (Biographical Series). http://msa.maryland.gov/megafile/msa/
    speccol/sc3500/sc3520/015800/015898/html/15898bio.html (accessed February 28,
    2018).
Hirsch, David, and Dan Van Haften. "The Structure of Reason."
    thestructureofreason.com (accessed February 28, 2018).
Jefferson, Thomas. "The Thomas Jefferson Papers." The Library of Congress.
    www.loc.gov/collections/thomas-jefferson-papers/about-this-collection (access
    February 28, 2018).
Literature & Latte. "Scrivener." www.literatureandlatte.com (accessed February 28,
    2018).
Neibuhr, Gustav. "Obama's 'Gettysburg Moment': For Us, the Living." The Huffington
    Post. huffingtonpost.com/gustav-niebuhr/obamas-gettysburg-moment-
    _b_808524.html (accessed February 28, 2018).
Obama, Barack. "Speeches and Remarks." The White House.
    obamawhitehouse.archives.gov/briefing-room/speeches-and-remarks (accessed
    February 28, 2018).
Siorvanes, Lucas. "Proclus." Oxford Bibliographies. www.oxfordbibliographies.com/
    view/document/obo-9780195389661/
    obo-9780195389661-0157.xml;jsessionid=C72370AC
    47815861BB864052161AAECE (accessed February 28, 2018).


Books

Adams, Charles Francis, ed. *The Works of John Adams, Second President of the United
    States.* 10 vols. Boston, MA: Little, Brown, and Company, 1865.
Adams, John. *Diary and Autobiography of John Adams.* 4 vols. Edited by L. H. Butterfield.
    Cambridge, MA: The Belknap Press of Harvard University Press, 1961.
Allen, Frank B., et al. *Geometry Student's Text, Part I, Prepared under the supervision of the
    Panel on Sample Textbooks of the School Mathematics Study Group.* New Haven, CT:
    Yale University Press, 1961.
Angle, Paul M., ed. *A Portrait of Abraham Lincoln in Letters by His Oldest Son.* Chicago, IL:
    Chicago Historical Society, 1968.
Arush, Rabbi Shalom. *The Garden of Emuna.* Third Edition. Jerusalem, Israel: Shut Shel
    Chessed Institutions, 2008.

Basler, Roy P., ed. *The Collected Works of Abraham Lincoln*. 9 vols. New Brunswick, NJ: Rutgers University Press, 1953.

Boyd, Julian P., ed., et al. *The Papers of Thomas Jefferson*. 43 vols. Princeton, NJ: Princeton University Press, 1950-2017.

Chase, Stuart. *The Tyranny of Words*. New York, NY: Harcourt, Brace, & World, Inc., 1938.

Cunningham, Noble E., Jr. *Jefferson vs. Hamilton: Confrontations that Shaped a Nation*. Boston, MA: Bedford/St. Martin's, 2000.

Euclid. *The Thirteen Books of Euclid's Elements. Translated from the text of Heiberg with Introduction and Commentary by Sir Thomas L. Heath, Volume I*. New York: Dover Publications, Inc., 1956.

Frank, John P. *Lincoln as a Lawyer*. Urbana, IL: University of Illinois Press, 1961.

Garner, Bryan A. *The Chicago Guide to Grammar, Usage, and Punctuation*. Chicago, IL: The University of Chicago Press, 2016.

Giffords, Gabrielle, and Mark Kelly. *Gabby: A Story of Courage and Hope*. New York, NY: Scribner, 2011.

Gow, James. *A Short History of Greek Mathematics*. New York, NY: Chelsea Publishing Company, 1968 (revised reprint from 1884).

Heath, Sir Thomas. *A History of Greek Mathematics, Volume I*. London: Oxford University Press, 1960 (reprinted from 1921).

Herndon, William H., and Jesse W. Weik. *Herndon's Lincoln*. Edited by Douglas L. Wilson and Rodney O. Davis. Urbana, IL: Knox College Lincoln Study Center and the University of Illinois Press, 2006.

Hirsch, David, and Dan Van Haften. *Abraham Lincoln and the Structure of Reason*. El Dorado Hills, CA: Savas Beatie, 2010.

Hirsch, David, and Dan Van Haften. *Barack Obama, Abraham Lincoln, and the Structure of Reason*. El Dorado Hills, CA: Savas Beatie, 2012.

Hirsch, David, and Dan Van Haften. *The Ultimate Guide to the Declaration of Independence*. El Dorado Hills, CA: Savas Beatie, 2017.

Hirsch, David, and Dan Van Haften. *The Ultimate Guide to the Gettysburg Address*. El Dorado Hills, CA: Savas Beatie, 2016.

Hogben, Lancelot. *Mathematics for the Million*. New York, NY: W. W. Norton & Company, Inc., 1937.

Holzer, Harold. *Lincoln at Cooper Union: The Speech that Made Abraham Lincoln President*. New York: Simon & Schuster, 2004.

Jefferson, Thomas, ed. and trans. *A Treatise on Political Economy, by the Count Destutt Tracy*. Georgetown, D.C.: Joseph Milligan, 1817.

Jefferson, Thomas. *The Autobiography of Thomas Jefferson*. Mineola, NY: Dover Publications, Inc., 2005.

Lehmann, Karl. *Thomas Jefferson: American Humanist*. New York, NY: The MacMillan Company, 1947.

Looney, J. Jefferson, ed. *The Papers of Thomas Jefferson: Retirement Series*. 14 vols. Princeton, NJ: Princeton University Press, 2004-2017.

Malone, Dumas. *The Story of the Declaration of Independence*. New York, NY: Oxford University Press, 1954.

Maziarz, Edward A., and Thomas Greenwood. *Greek Mathematical Philosophy*. New York, NY: Frederick Ungar Publishing Company, 1968.

McLuhan, Marshall. *Understanding Media: The Extensions of Man.* New York, NY: McGraw-Hill Book Company, 1964.

Miers, Earl S., ed. *Lincoln Day by Day: A Chronology 1809-1865.* Dayton, OH: Morningside, 1991.

Mueller, Ian. *Philosophy of Mathematics and Deductive Structure in Euclid's* Elements. Cambridge, MA: The MIT Press, 1981.

Newkirk, Garrett. *Lincoln Lessons for Today.* New York, NY: Duffield and Company, 1921.

Oldroyod, Osborn H. *The Lincoln Memorial: Album-Immortelles.* Boston, MA: D. L. Guernsey, 1882.

Parton, James. *Life of Thomas Jefferson.* Boston, MA: James R. Osgood and Company, 1874.

Patrick, David, ed. *Chambers's Biographical Dictionary.* Philadelphia, PA: J. B Lippincott Company, 1898.

Peters, Richard, ed. *The Public Statutes at Large of the United States of America, Volume I.* Boston, MA: Charles C. Little and James Brown, 1845.

Peterson, Merrill D., ed. *Visitors to Monticello.* Charlottesville, VA: University Press of Virginia, 1989.

Proclus. *A Commentary on the First Book of Euclid's Elements, Translated, with Introduction and notes, by Glenn R. Morrow.* Princeton, NJ: Princeton University Press, 1970.

Rankin, Henry B. *Intimate Character Sketches of Abraham Lincoln.* Philadelphia, PA: J. B. Lippincott Company, 1924.

Rankin, Henry B. *Personal Recollections of Abraham Lincoln.* New York, NY: G.P. Putnam's Sons, 1916.

Strunk, William, Jr., and E. B. White. *The Elements of Style.* 3rd ed. New York, NY: MacMillan Publishing Company, 1979.

United States Congress. *Biographical Directory of the United States Congress 1774-2005.* Washington, D. C.: United States Government Printing Office, 2005.

United States Continental Congress. *Journals of the Continental Congress 1774-1789, Volume V. 1776 June 5 - October 8.* Washington: Government Printing Office, 1906.

Wanamaker, R. M. *The Voice of Lincoln.* New York, NY: Charles Scribner's Sons, 1918.

White, Ronald C., Jr. *A. Lincoln: A Biography.* New York, NY: Random House, 2009.

Whitney, Henry C. *Lincoln the Citizen.* Edited by Marion Mills Miller. New York, NY: The Baker & Taylor Company, 1908.

Wilson, Douglas L. *Lincoln's Sword: The Presidency and the Power of Words.* New York, NY: Vintage Books, 2006.

## Journals & Magazine Articles

Arnold, Isaac N. "Reminiscences of the Illinois Bar: 1840 – Lincoln and Douglas as Orators and Lawyers." *Illinois Bar Journal* 47 (1959): 572-578.

Hadley, Arthur T. "The Meaning and Purpose of Secondary Education." *The School Review* X No. 10 (1902): 738.

Reid, Ronald F. "Newspaper Response to the Gettysburg Address." *Quarterly Journal of Speech* 53 (February 1967): 52.

# Index

Note: The letter "d" indicates a demarcation.

# Authors

**David Hirsch** is an attorney in Des Moines, Iowa. He has a BS from Michigan State University and a JD, with distinction, from the University of Iowa College of Law. He clerked for an Iowa Supreme Court Justice from 1973 to 1974. In addition to a full-time law practice, Hirsch was a columnist for the American Bar Association Journal for over a decade. Hirsch is admitted to practice in all Iowa state trial and appellate courts, plus: United States Supreme Court, United States Court of Appeals for the Eighth Circuit, United States District Court for the Southern District of Iowa, United States District Court for the Northern District of Iowa, United States Court of Claims, United States Tax Court.

**Dan Van Haften** lives in Batavia, Illinois. He has BS, with high honor, and MS degrees in mathematics from Michigan State University, and a Ph.D. in electrical engineering from Stevens Institute of Technology. He began his career at AT&T Bell Laboratories in 1970, and retired from Alcatel-Lucent in 2007. He worked on telecommunication software development and system testing.

David Hirsch and Dan Van Haften also authored *Abraham Lincoln and the Structure of Reason* (2010), *Barack Obama, Abraham Lincoln, and the Structure of Reason* (2012), *The Ultimate Guide to the Gettysburg Address* (2016), and *The Ultimate Guide to the Declaration of Independence* (2017).

www.thestructureofreason.com